Cures and Chaos

The Life & Times of Dr. Vincent Hume and His Impact on a Frontier Alaska Town

Joseph Homme

PO Box 221974 Anchorage, Alaska 99522-1974
books@publicationconsultants.com—www.publicationconsultants.com

ISBN 978-1-59433-060-5

Library of Congress Catalog Card Number: 2007925471

Copyright 2007 by Joseph Homme
—First Edition—

Manufactured in the United States of America.

For Vinnie

The past is never dead, it's not even past.
William Faulkner

4

Contents

Introduction

A mong early primitive peoples, disease was thought to be caused by malevolent spirits. To bring relief to the sick, medicine-men or shaman were employed to do battle with the spirits through the use of ritual and magic. For their efforts, communities accorded these practitioners great respect. Mixed with this respect was a little fear, for if shaman were capable of conjuring up good spirits, perhaps they were also capable of summoning evil ones. The shaman did little to dispel such notions. To further their aims, these medicine-men formed their own hierarchy and maintained for themselves an air of mystery. They were a formidable group.

The connection between spirits and disease eventually gave way to science-based concepts. Though medicine shifted away from its spiritual beginnings, public perception still linked the two, for it appeared that only two entities were capable of healing the sick: God and doctors. Such beliefs continued and even expanded into the mid-20th century when medical miracles seemed so plentiful. For whether one believed that doctors achieved cures solely on their own, or that they were a conduit for the healing hand of God, the profession inspired reverence.

Beneath the protective mantle of this pedestal profession, however, reality and perception diverged dramatically. In reality, doctors were decidedly human. Any public perception that held otherwise placed doctors at risk of professional or personal failure.

1

Born to Run

The Glasgow Rain

Dora Brogden Hume had had enough of Scotland. The people were fine, but for her, the general environment was lacking. Her family, consisting of husband Alexander, called Alick, and children Frank and Medora, had resided for nearly two years in a four room flat, much smaller than they were used to when Dora suggested it was time to leave Glasgow and return to their native Canada. She never fully adapted to the new culture, the food, and certainly not to the weather; in one winter it had rained for seventy days straight. She had kept count. On top of it all, she was pregnant and wanted to return to familiar surroundings and the proximity to family. And so it was decided. Alick gave notice at the tea firm where he was employed as head accountant. The children, who found the entire Scottish experience to be an adventure, left their respective schools, Frank from Mount Florida and Medora from Queen's Park. They bade farewell to their friends from the neighborhood and church and embarked upon the Dominion Line steamship, the *S/S Scotsman,* bound for Montreal.

The nine-day trip was another adventure thoroughly enjoyed by the children, but much less so by Alick, who suffered from extreme seasickness. In Montreal, the family boarded a westbound Canadian Pacific Railway train for the long trans-Canada trek to Calgary, Alberta. In Calgary, Dora and Medora stayed with Dora's mother to await the birth of the baby. Alick and Frank continued on to Golden, British Columbia where they boarded a riverboat that took them up the Columbia River and landed them on the shore of a large, remote ranch that Alick had been hired to manage. Back in Calgary, the baby arrived on July 5, 1898 and was christened John Alexander Hume. Mother and daughter were anxious to join the men at the ranch so with month-old John in tow, they journeyed west to Golden, from there taking the small steamer, *Duchess,* up the Columbia.

At the ranch. From left Dora, John, and Alick Hume. (*Hume family collection*)

If Glasgow had been something of a culture shock, so was the ranch—in the opposite extreme. Alick, Dora, and the children had moved from an enormous bustling seaport city to the frontier of western Canada. There they found no amenities, schools, or even neighbors. They were completely isolated, but at least there was plenty to do. The horses, cows, sheep, and chickens needed daily care and feeding. In the summer and fall, crops were raised, harvested, and stored to provide winter feed for the stock. The family's own winter food stores were also to be obtained. There were shearing and butchering duties. Fences, corrals, and buildings were constructed, and existing structures maintained. The Hume's successful stay at the remote ranch infused them with a pioneer spirit and a sense of accomplishment. But their tenure there was limited by practicality. As young John neared school age, his parents were keenly aware of his need for a formal education. So the decision was made to move to town.

Lacombe

One of the benefits of service in the Northwest Mounted Police was the award of a section of land. Past officer Ed Barnett's property of choice was in a grassy valley rich in agricultural resources located in central Alberta at roughly the midpoint between Edmonton and Calgary. Here he established a homestead in 1883. Seven years later, the Canadian Pacific Railway (CPR) laid tracks near the Barnett homestead as it constructed a route between the two cities. Travelers who had previously passed through the valley on their way to someplace else began to see promise in the area, and people came to stay. The CPR noticed the trend and constructed a siding to serve the new residents. It contained donated railcars which functioned as a rail station and a post office. The siding's official name was Siding No. 12. The locals called it Barnett's Siding. As the area continued steady growth and developed into a farming community and business center, it needed a proper official name; Siding No. 12 would no longer do. As was often the case in those days, the railroad had the final word, naming the community Lacombe after Father Albert Lacombe, a Catholic Missionary credited for bringing peace to the region's warring Cree and Blackfoot Indian tribes.

The Hume family arrived just as Lacombe had earned the status of a certified town though it had the look of a frontier boomtown: white-washed frame structures, wood buildings completely unadorned by paint, and boardwalks which skirted buildings with tall false fronts. The exception

Downtown Lacombe, B.C. (*Maski-Pitoon Historical Society*)

was the Merchants Bank, a grand brick and stone structure that graced the so-called Flatiron business district. The bank gave a confidence that Lacombe had "arrived" and was here to stay. And there was a school in Lacombe. Nelson School was a one room, single story, white frame schoolhouse in which John Hume enrolled in 1905. Alick opened a real estate agency on what stood for Lacombe's main street, Barnett Avenue. Frank, much older than his brother John, was off surveying for the CPR, work that took him away from Lacombe, south to Gleichen and Bassano. Lacombe was as the Humes had hoped:

abounding educational and business opportunities, and friendly, lively residents.

Sometimes the townsfolk were a little too lively. The Victoria
Hotel was the principal lodging place for visitors, its bar the
meeting place for locals and visitors alike. Occasionally the
revelry got out of hand at the Victoria Bar with patrons entering
the tavern on horseback. Elements of the Wild West remained.
Lacombe's main drawback was its habit of burning down with
shocking regularity. The spread of fire was due, in part, to the
dry prairie grasses growing in the streets and alleys next to
the tinderbox-dry wood buildings. Firefighting efforts were met
with limited success. After one fire swept through the Flatiron
district, leaving only the Merchants Bank and little else in its
wake, the town council took bold action. The council decreed
under a bylaw that all new Lacombe commercial buildings must
be of brick construction. Further, the bylaw stated, older existing commercial structures must be covered with a brick veneer.
Though this was an audacious government action, specifying
the use of a particular type of building material and requiring
the costly retrofitting of existing buildings, there was little out-
cry from the business community, for the people had grown
weary of the fires. As a result of the new requirements, the
local brick industry flourished. A number of yards competed
for construction spending. Alick was an investor in the brick
business when, in addition to his other ventures, he and a partner purchased the Fletcher Brick Yard west of Lacombe. The
council's brick mandate worked. Fires still occurred but did not
spread to surrounding structures as before.

Lacombe continued to grow and provide amenities to its citizens; amenities that would in short order become necessities, such
as electric power—first generated from a dam on Blind Man River
and later, more reliably, from a steam engine power plant. The
area was recognized as an agricultural center and was awarded
a Dominion Experimental Station to improve techniques in livestock care and breeding and to increase crop production.

The Humes also had a variety of recreational opportunities
at their disposal, including the popular picnic area at Gull Lake
where a family could take in the yacht races or dance on the
rooftops of the lake's resort hotels. Movies were shown in town
on Saturday nights and grocery stores remained open until

midnight to serve the moviegoing crowd, giving the nights a festive atmosphere. Barnstorming Negro League baseball teams journeyed north to Lacombe, treating the locals to some of the highest quality baseball played anywhere. Children made their own fun with games like "Shinny," a somewhat brutal form of hockey played without benefit of protective equipment, with crude sticks, and a tin can puck. This popular game was, supposedly, named for the wounds and scarring inflicted upon the shins of its participants. By 1915 John Hume was past the point of engaging in youthful games of Shinny. He had recently completed all the formal education the town had to offer and had entered the workforce as a bank clerk at Lacombe's Union Bank. As a young adult he was slight in physical stature, standing a little over 5'8" with a slim build, brown hair, and blue eyes. He was very intelligent and displayed his father's formidable abilities with numbers and managing money. He was eager to get started with his life, but world events would conflict with his personal ambitions.

World War I

Though fifteen years apart in age, brothers Frank and John Hume had a close relationship. The remoteness of the Columbia River ranch had made the family members mutually dependent for social interaction, the ranch's success, and even their own survival. Frank was the kind of big brother John could depend on, and John knew it. Really they all knew it. Frank was an admirable person who would be proven even more so in the years to come. As an adult he stood six feet in height, possessing a slim build. He had dark brown hair, gray eyes, and a fair complexion. He was widely considered to be very handsome. His formal education had more or less ended after the family's stay in Glasgow, but Frank never let that lack of formal schooling interfere with his endeavors. He started a self-directed course of study in the field of engineering, getting practical experience in the field, earning a living, and studying the technical and theoretical aspects through reading. By this method he merited the position of Civil Engineer, specializing in irrigation. He was indeed a self-made man. For John, Frank was simply the older brother he would always look up to. In February of 1916, when Frank enlisted in the Canadian Overseas Expeditionary Force (CEF) it was only a matter of time before John followed.

John's decision to enlist was not solely in response to his brother's. Although Canada was essentially a non-militaristic country, its allegiance to Mother England was very strong—so strong that the defense of the Isles was a matter of Canadian national pride. That's the way they saw it in Lacombe too, a town which contributed, proportionally, a large number of soldiers to the European war effort. John Hume was one of them when he enlisted in November of 1916 at the age of eighteen.

For much of the war, the Germans occupied Passchendaele, Belgium and a ridge that cut through the country on an arc from Passchendaele to Messines. The heavily fortified German high ground, in the area of Passchendaele, overlooked what had been gently rolling grazing land. It didn't look much like grazing land by the fall of 1917; instead it resembled a moonscape, a wasteland with few discernible landmarks, utterly barren. It was about to get much worse. In two previous clashes referred to as 1st and 2nd Ypres, the battles had been launched by the Germans; this time it was the Allies who went on the offensive. In late July, prior to the Allied attack, British guns shelled the German lines for ten days, expending more than 4,000,000 shells. What the shelling accomplished was not what was intended. The pasture land had earlier been a swamp; only through the construction of a complex drainage system had the low-lying soils been reclaimed. With the bombardment, the system was destroyed, and the water had no place go. The Allies had not understood how fragile was the land their troops were about to cross in battle. Then the heaviest rains in thirty years began. Allied tanks were rendered useless in the quagmire. The troops had to advance on their own without the benefit of tank cover and the tanks' ability to ride down barbed wire. Across a field of knee- to thigh-deep mud, channeled by the impassable rows of barbed wire went the Allied troops, into the German killing zone.

The fighting continued this way for months. It was the war's last great battle of attrition, the Allies believing they could afford to lose more soldiers than the Germans. With the loss of so many Allied troops with little result, the Canadians were called in. Fighting along with the British, the Canadians inherited a mud-filled battlefield that had worsened since the opening assault months earlier. Vast areas resembled quicksand, where some soldiers and horses, unable to free themselves, drowned in the muck. It was a rank, filthy field of death, and for the Canadians there was something more. Gas. For the first time, the Germans employed mustard gas in their explosive shells against the Canadian forces. Mustard gas was far more dangerous than the previously used chlorine gas. It caused blistering where it contacted skin and when inhaled it caused respiratory ailments that could result in death. But it was not an effective killing weapon; its primary use was inflicting injury on soldiers, thereby depleting the enemy's resources in the care of the wounded.

This was the state of battle Frank Hume encountered at 3rd Ypres. His involvement was his own choice. After his enlistment in the 172nd Battalion of the Canadian Overseas Expeditionary Force, he had been sent to England where he transferred to the 47th Battalion of the CEF, promoted to Sergeant, and sent to France. He hoped he would see action in Europe, but no such action occurred. In an effort to reach the front, he took a demotion in grade and was sent forward participating in the combat at Lens, France. His next assignment was in Belgium where he and the soldiers of D Company reached the battlefront several days before their planned inclusion in the fighting. This was common at Ypres, as the forward march over miles of duck boards in full combat gear (rain-soaked great coats alone could weigh more than forty pounds) was such an arduous task that soldiers had to rest before entering battle. It wasn't actually rest. The days preceding combat were used to hand-transport rations, clothing, ammunition, and other supplies. Another task that fell to these "resting" soldiers was the periodic formation of burial parties, sent out to claim the dead while under fire, and inter them. Frank, who returned to his post as sergeant, often worked in and supervised the burial details.

Before going to the front, Frank was joined in Ypres by his brother John. As D Company moved forward, it experienced very heavy shelling and machine-gun fire from the Germans. On October 26th and 27th the Company was at the front and had advanced its position to occupy a former enemy-held trench on a low ridge southwest of the Augustus Wood position. The shelling intensified and an order was given to abandon the trench line. Frank was directing the evacuation of his troops when he was hit by a German sniper's bullet. He was still alive when John found him. Aware that wounded soldiers left waiting for stretchers on the battlefield seldom survived, John carried his brother to safety, under fire, over the muddy, shell-cratered battlefield to the relative safety of the Canadian lines, where Frank lingered for several days before finally succumbing to his wounds on October 31, 1917. In addition to the emotional injury of the loss of his older brother, John had been gassed.

Back to Lacombe

The period of convalescence associated with mustard gas poisoning depended on the severity of the burns. The large blisters from skin contact were prone to infection, especially in the unsanitary conditions of the battlefront. Victims were usually transported elsewhere to recover. During his hospital stay, John learned that the battle of 3rd Ypres, or Passchendaele as it would also be known, lasted another week after his brother's death, and ended in an Allied victory. He also learned of Frank's burial in Belgium, some ten miles from the battle site. John returned home to Lacombe alone.

John's discharge from the Canadian Army came in February, 1919 in Vancouver, British Columbia. The sadness he felt for the loss of his brother continued to weigh on him. In speaking of Frank, John declared that his older brother was the bravest man he ever knew. In Lacombe, John found other veterans who'd had horrific war experiences. A number of those former soldiers had difficulties resuming their civilian lives. Some returned from Europe with the dreaded influenza virus which brought sickness and death to others in the small town. The effects of the war would continue, not only for the former servicemen, but also for the grieving families of the seventy-six Lacombe soldiers who had been killed in action. It was a heavy toll for a small, rural area.

The healing power of time serves whole communities as well as individuals. The town, though mindful of its losses, began to heal and prosperity beckoned. For John Hume, the healing began when he took notice of a girl he had known for some time, Clara Harrington. He and Clara had both attended Nelson

School in Lacombe. Clara's father, William C. Harrington, built, owned, and operated the imposing brick Empress Hotel. Theirs was a business family. The Harringtons had previously built the St. James Hotel in Edmonton, after owning and operating a produce market in Winnipeg, Manitoba, the city where Clara was

born in 1895. John's interest in Clara had little to do with business—far from it. He admired the very nature of the girl; she was a pure joy to be around. Clara was bubbly, outgoing, and seemed to literally sparkle. She was diminutive, standing only about 4'9" with a slim, athletic build. She was self-conscious about her height and always wore shoes that provided a lift. Even her house slippers contained a wedged heel. Her hair was naturally curly and she generally wore it up. She was considered an attractive woman. Clara's upbeat and sometimes

The diminutive Clara Harrington. (*Maski-Pitoon Historical Society*)

comic personality was the perfect foil to John's growing seriousness, as he turned his interests to matters of the business world. She was drawn to him for his intelligence and strength. He was kind and generous. He was an entrepreneur, going places and doing things. They married on January 27, 1921.

Traveling Man

Clara gave birth to the couple's first child, Vincent Harrington Hume, or Vinnie as he was called, on October 31, 1921. John had wanted to name his first born son in honor of his older brother, but since the birth occurred on the fourth anniversary of Frank's death, that no longer seemed appropriate. Vinnie's birth, like any new addition to a family, opened a transitional period in the newlyweds' lives. John's lifestyle of travel and business, which had once seemed interesting and exciting to Clara, now made him an absent spouse and father. At times it seemed that Lacombe was but a stop on his route. In 1923, a second child was born. This male child received his uncle's name, Frank Hume, and was called Frankie. The birth was another joyous event but it tied Clara down even more while John was away. For the family to have any hope of being together, Clara and the boys had to move closer to John's new base of operation. Within the year, they were in Anyox, British Columbia.

Anyox was a mining town founded by the Gransby Mining

The brothers Hume. Vinnie 3½ and Frankie 1½.
(*Hume family collection*)

and Smelting Company as a center for smelting the area's rich copper ore. More of an industrial complex than a town, it was high on smoke and other airborne particles, and low on services and aesthetics. But Clara and the boys weren't in Anyox for the amenities—they were there in the interest of family unity. Unfortunately, family unity wasn't happening, at least not to the degree hoped. Another child, daughter Doreen, was born there in 1925. For Clara, it seemed John was only around long enough to father more children before he moved on once more. He supported the family well enough financially, but she couldn't help wondering about the allure of the road and with whom her husband might be doing business. As she was not one given to complaining, all she did was worry—worry, and raise the children. In 1927 it was time to move again, this time because Vinnie was nearing school age and a proper education wasn't available in Anyox. The family moved to Vancouver, British

Columbia. Vinnie started school in 1928 at Duncan Catholic School, located in the town of Duncan in the Cowichan Valley of southern Vancouver Island. It was a boarding school for boys, and while it offered excellent educational opportunities, its standards of discipline were sometimes enforced in a harsh manner to which Vinnie was unaccustomed. He did not like life at the boarding school. Life at home was difficult as well.

Hard Times

John and Clara decided to divorce. They had been separated a great deal of their married life, and that separation contributed to John's interest in another woman. For Clara, John's affair wasn't as devastating as it might have been—in her mind she had been abandoned years before. The terrible truth was that she was left to raise the children on her own without the level of financial support she and the children had previously enjoyed. Options were very limited for a divorcee with three young children at the start of the Great Depression. Child care services and training programs for women were virtually non-existent. The best chance a single mother had was to remarry.

Grover

Grover Bates, an American, was a business associate of John Hume. Through that association he had come to know Clara. With the Hume's divorce came the opportunity for him to get to know Clara a little better.

For his time, Grover was a man of the world. In an era when most people journeyed only a few miles from their birthplace, Grover was amazingly well traveled. He was born to James and Emma Bates in Wichita, Kansas in the fall of 1889, the youngest of five children. The family moved to Oklahoma's Noble County by the summer of 1900, where James found employment as a farm laborer. Grover's interest in cowboying led him to leave home while in his teens to work as a ranch hand on Charlie Collins' spread in Sheridan County, Wyoming. From his cowboy days forward, Grover's choice of occupations and living locales frequently changed. He seemed to always be in search of new opportunities and experiences. It was no mere pedestrian lifestyle; he paid attention and learned along the way, picking up valuable information concerning human nature that would serve him well later. He was well-read too, especially poetry, which gave him a certain bearing, an impression of high-mindedness. When his journeys took him to the northwest where he found work in the logging camps, he entertained his fellow workers during the Saturday night talent shows with poems he had memorized, including James Whitcomb Riley's epic poem *Squire Hawkins's Story,* which took nearly fifteen minutes to recite. He traveled to Pennsylvania, and at some point he was married, but only for a short time. He lived in Bismarck, North Dakota, where he was employed in the newspaper business with Compton Brothers of Finley, Ohio. While in Bismarck he registered for the draft but claimed an exemption from service citing a physical disability—a "bad left eye." He made the first of two voyages to China shortly after the war's end. Of all his occupational pursuits, sales were best suited to Grover's natural talents. He could sell just about anything. He was working in sales when he met Clara.

Grover in China. (*Hume family collection*)

To Grover's way of thinking, Clara was a woman wronged. His affection for her was genuine, and his feelings were reciprocated.

Grover was a worldly, intelligent man. He was handsome, always immaculately groomed, even dapper. He was careful with money and was a nondrinker. He had a stable personality. In Grover, Clara found a man who wanted to be with her, or at least wanted to have her with him in the course of his travels. Grover and Clara were married in December, 1934. It was an added bonus that Grover genuinely loved Clara's children. He was especially fond of Doreen, whom he called "Buttercup," and of Frankie. Vinnie was a harder sell for Grover. The eldest Hume child viewed Grover with a certain sense of resentment, perhaps transferring his feelings from the divorce to the newcomer of the family. Vinnie's age of adolescent rebellion coincided with Grover's arrival in his mother's life. His step-father was an easy target for Vinnie's youthful angst, but Grover was not without his frustrating ways either. His often opinionated manner could squelch useful discourse. Grover often said, "There are two ways of doing things. The Bates way and the wrong way." Vinnie found this aggravating. Grover and Vinnie possessed the strongest personalities in the family—personalities that would continue to conflict.

Kitsilano Jr./Sr. High. (*Leonard Frank photo, Vancouver Public Library, VPL 5417*)

Back to School

Though Vinnie was still attending a Catholic School which did not appeal to him, at least it wasn't a boarding school. St. Augustine's School in Vancouver was a three story Victorian style structure built in 1911 at the corner of Arbutus and Seventh Avenue. The facility's first and third floors consisted of a parish hall and church respectively. The middle floor housed the school's eight grades, divided into four classrooms. Vinnie attended the school for four years, transferring to Kitsilano Junior/Senior High School in Vancouver in 1935. He was a bright student with an attitude similar to his mother's—easygoing and cheerful. He was a bit of a scamp in school, possessing a quick wit and boyish mischievousness.

During these early teen years, Vinnie experienced a major illness. He contracted scarlet fever and had a severe reaction. The symptoms—sore throat, rash, and fever—were so intense that Vinnie had to be hospitalized. He was placed in isolation because of the contagious nature of the disease. To ease the fever, his head was shaved. Little else could be done for him. The only treatment for scarlet fever at that time was rest. Though the effects of the illness were minimal, the loneliness he felt in the isolation ward, when even his family was not allowed to visit him, had a lasting effect on him. Vinnie's brother Frankie was ill with scarlet fever too, though no one knew it at the time. He did not react as strongly, nor recover as well as his older brother. The symptoms were so mild that Frankie was never diagnosed with the disease. In his case, the initial streptococcal infection of scarlet fever was followed about three weeks later by rheumatic fever. Again the symptoms were mild, and this too went undiagnosed. From this point forward, Frankie experienced general ill health; a vague sickness always seemed present. Later he was diagnosed, in retrospect, with rheumatic fever when it was discovered that his heart valves had been deformed by the disease.

Like all boys his age, events of the world captured Vinnie's imagination. In those mid-Depression, pre-World War II years with so little good news available, a new project was heralded. It was the subject of radio broadcasts, newspaper articles, and newsreels—the very stuff of adventure; American families were being sent north to tame the frontier of Alaska.

2

The Colony

A New Deal

Having campaigned hard against Herbert Hoover with claims that the incumbent president was a leader unable to meet the challenges of a great national Depression, the new president, Franklin Delano Roosevelt, had received his mandate. The signal was clear. Americans wanted no more to do with plodding, ineffective attempts at relief and reform. Roosevelt almost immediately put into action a series of measures designed to stem the skyrocketing unemployment rate and get Americans back to work. Changes to the bureaucracy were massive, with program after program implemented in an attempt to stimulate the economy and restore a measure of hope in the people.

One of those programs fell under the management of the Federal Emergency Relief Administration (FERA). It called for the organization of rural farming cooperatives. A list of possible locations was developed during the program's planning stages. In 1934, Roosevelt instructed FERA officials to add the Territory of Alaska to the list. The exact location was in the territory's south-central region in an area called the Matanuska Valley.

The Matanuska Valley was chosen for a number of reasons. The area showed excellent potential for agriculture. This meant a substantially increased likelihood of success for the program's intended subsistence lifestyle. Additionally, any surplus produce could be sold in the nearby city of Anchorage. The new farming corporation would thereby serve as a fresher and less expensive source of food, freeing south-central Alaska of its dependence on Outside shipping centers.

Planning for the new settlement, or "colony" as it would be called, was undertaken rather hastily, as many projects were in the heady, early days of the Roosevelt Administration. With land acquisition underway, data was collected in an effort to design roads, homes, barns, and a new town. Profiles of ideal candidates for the program were outlined. Building material sources were researched. Livestock and farm machinery were acquired for the colonists. Other agencies were brought in or created to help, including the California Emergency Relief Administration (CERA), and the Alaska Rural Rehabilitation Corporation (ARRC). The logistics were endless, time wasn't. Colonization began in early 1935.

The Chosen

A great many families vied for the chance to journey north and become colonists. Even considering the harsh realities of Depression times, a surprising many wanted to go, trading the only life they had ever known for the unknown. No friends, no extended family, and it was so very far away. "What if we don't like it?" they must have wondered. "We will be leaving here with nothing and coming back with even less," was probably often the answer. Still, 204 selected families seized the opportunity. For if nothing else, frontiers provide a new chance, a chance to be part of something big. Maybe a chance to prove something on a personal level, too. The new colonists felt great fortune at having been chosen.

The Journey North

All packed up, the colonists set out on their journey, cross-country, by rail. Accompanying them were news correspondents and photographers. At stops along the way, they were celebrated as modern-day pioneers, the very embodiment of what made the country great. The colonists were the subject of speeches, parades, and other gala events. Scores of Americans turned out to see and greet these adventuresome souls. Morale among the families ran high. Colonists who shipped out of San Francisco were even treated to a U.S. Navy battleship escort for a portion of their sea journey. Upon arrival in Seward, Alaska, the colonists boarded railcars for the trip to Anchorage where they were treated to still more festivities.

From Anchorage, the train took them to the Palmer Railroad Station in the Matanuska Valley.

The Party's Over

The Talkeetna and Chugach Mountain Ranges serve as a border to the Matanuska Valley. The region's topography and soil conditions are a mixed lot. Elevations run from mountainous to marshy. Rich farming soils may reach six feet in depth in some areas, but just inches in others. Spruce, cottonwood, and birch trees, somewhat slight in girth, are plentiful in number. Lakes and creeks are numerous. Two large glacier-fed rivers, the Matanuska and Knik, run through the valley to Cook Inlet. The town of Palmer lies just west of the Matanuska River, forty miles north of Anchorage. When the first wave of colonists detrained in Palmer in May of 1935, they found themselves surrounded by snowcapped mountains, the likes of which most had never seen. As it was still early spring, the natural surroundings were bleak and colorless. Their lodgings were nearby; a newly constructed tent city—row upon row of stark white canvas shelters set up in a hayfield. As these families settled into their temporary abodes, still more colonists were on their way to Palmer. Within two weeks, all had arrived.

We Didn't Think It Would Be Like This

The colonists had much to see and learn, for it was all so different, beginning with the long Alaska days of summer. They found an amazing abundance of fish and game. Who could have imagined the forest's thick jungle-like undergrowth? The summer was temperate, without the stifling humidity of "back home." No snakes. No tornados. Not even a real thunderstorm to scare the little ones. But there were bugs—mosquitoes so numerous that they seemed at times a curse of Biblical proportion. And there was dust. Dust so fine that it could find its way into anything, especially through drafty tents. Then there was the mud. It didn't take much water when added to fine glacial soil to make a real mess. It was impossible to keep anything clean.

These conditions made the wait to move into their finished homes seem even longer. Surely, the construction should have been progressing faster. Some wondered if their homes would be completed by winter. Construction site visits added fuel to the colonists' apprehension. Not all the crews worked in an efficient manner, and the quality of craftsmanship was unsatisfactory. Many families began questioning their involvement with the program. Quite naturally, feelings of homesickness intensified. Still they persevered. The conditions weren't intolerable. Not yet.

Voices from the Wilderness

The children were sick, and not enough was being done about it. Illnesses had started on the trip north, with families traveling in close proximity to one another. Viruses, colds, and the flu moved quickly in cramped quarters. In Palmer, the sicknesses continued due, in part, to the unsanitary and primitive living conditions. Cases of measles and scarlet fever were identified, and the colonists feared a full-scale epidemic. Then tragedy struck. Three children succumbed to illness. The only on-site medical staff consisted of one overworked nurse. In desperation, a group of mothers wired Eleanor Roosevelt in a plea for medical assistance for the colony. The mothers' voices were heard. A team of investigators traveled to Palmer to ascertain the extent of the problem. They quickly learned that the content of the telegram was not an overstatement. Action was swift. From Anchorage, by rail, came three nurses and Dr. Earl Albrecht. They came to heal the sick and restore peace of mind in the beleaguered colony.

3

Across the Border

What's In a Name?

Vinnie knew something was afoot. The family was preparing for yet another move—that much was plain. But why were they moving, and what was the big hurry? To top it off, a wall of silence had gone up, which only added to the mystery and confusion. It wasn't even clear where they were going. When the move came, in mid-1936, it wasn't very far from Vancouver, but it was to a new country. Quickly and quietly they relocated to Seattle, Washington. There was another matter too. For some reason, Vinnie's mother and step-father, Clara and Grover Bates, insisted the three children change their last names. They said it was so that John Hume wouldn't know of their whereabouts. The reason given for the name change seemed a little sketchy, but the emphasis placed on the request was not. It was a demand. The children accepted the change. They would be known as Vinnie Somers, Frankie Somers, and Doreen Somers. There were no legal proceedings to make the name change official. That would have foiled the true objective.

Not a Second Time

While her love for her children was never in question, neither was Clara's relationship with Grover—it was one of great depth and strength. Perceiving that her first marriage had ended, in part, because of her inability to travel with her husband John, Clara did not want the situation repeated. Grover was a man on the move, and Clara would accompany him on his travels, even if it meant more separations from her children.

On The Road

Grover was a traveling salesman working both door-to-door for companies like Fuller Brush and in commercial sales as a distributor for Chilton's, selling manuals to garages and automotive parts stores. It was not an easy way to make a living. With Clara along, it was at least tolerable, and Grover was glad to have her. The children were thankful to have each other during these long periods of separation from their mother and step-father. Among the children an incredible, lasting bond was forged. Vinnie, Frankie, and Doreen's shared experience not only brought them closer but also taught them to look after one another. The times when they were under the care of others varied from acceptable to extremely difficult. They were often dropped off at the homes of Grover's relatives and friends, and on at least one occasion, at an orphanage. Sometimes a family was willing to take on the responsibility of boarding one or two of the children, but not all three. In these instances the younger two children were kept together while Vinnie was placed elsewhere. Vinnie felt abandoned during these times, resenting any arrangement that left him with people he didn't know. Not only was the environment ever-changing, but so was the level of care provided, including the most basic of necessities—nourishment. When staying with one family, the children were so ill-fed that Vinnie and Frankie were driven to steal bottled milk from porches. Sometimes the host families were rigid, intolerant, or even abusive. While Frankie and Doreen seemed fairly adaptable to most of these situations, Vinnie was less resilient. For Vinnie this was no way to live, and in his estimation, his parents should have realized the hazards of leaving their children so often with so many different families.

The all important adolescent social scene offered little relief. The children were never in any one place long enough to develop a single lasting friendship. Nor were they in a region long enough to learn the area's culture. For the kids, school experiences, the social and cultural mecca of youth, came and went at a rapid pace. Vinnie started his first year in the States at Madison School in Seattle but was not allowed to finish. Instead the family moved mid-year to Los Angeles where Vinnie attended Virgil Junior High School, where he graduated from the ninth grade. He spent his sophomore year at Classen High

School in Oklahoma City, Oklahoma. But, at last, after moving the family three times in two years, Grover and Clara seemed to run out of moves and a normal home, social and school life—really the children's first—was in the offing. When the family settled in San Antonio, Texas, Vinnie spent his junior and senior years at Hot Wells High School.

Deep in the Heart of Texas

At 5'7", Vinnie's slender build didn't make him a young man of Texas-size proportions. He didn't find success playing high school basketball or football, practically a social handicap for boys in the Lone Star State. He actually was a good athlete, blessed with excellent coordination, and was an asset to the tennis squad, but tennis was, at best, a minor sport. He was a good looking kid— the girls thought him cute—with dark brown hair and blue eyes, but he also looked a little young for his age, not a good thing when attempting to appear mature and worldly at seventeen. Fortunately, Vinnie had something else going for him— that intangible attribute called charisma. It was a positive force within him that seemed to at-

Vinnie and friend enjoying sports afield. (*Hume family collection*)

tract just about everyone. He was always cheerful, sporting about the biggest grin anyone had ever seen—so big in fact that his eyes would close to mere slits when he flashed a smile. He was intelligent, but in no way bookish, which made him seem even cooler. He was smart without trying. Some thought him a little cocky, not in a brash way, but in keeping with his adventuresome spirit. He wasn't a big risk taker, but did give the impression of fearlessness in his approach to life.

Hot Wells High School stood at the corner of Hot Wells Boulevard and Russi Street in San Antonio. Originally constructed in 1912, the building underwent a number of renovations and additions prior to Vinnie's enrollment. Hot Wells High, during the period of Vinnie's attendance, was a two story Spanish-styled buff-colored brick building. The roof had barrel shaped Spanish red clay tiles. The ground floor contained a freshman classroom, cafeteria, science lab, restrooms, and storage facilities. The second floor held another freshman classroom as well as one classroom each for the sophomore, junior, and senior students. Also on this top story were the administrative office, records office, and student study hall. On the school grounds were asphalt tennis courts and a separate building which contained a gymnasium. The athletic teams, the Hot Wells Blue Devils, sported the school's blue and gold colors.

A trio of Hot Wells lettermen. Vinnie center. (*Hume family collection*)

The all-girl drum and bugle corps pep squad was called the Scotch Lassie Patrol. Student government had been established, as well as a National Honor Society group. It was a small school with active participation from the students. The kids liked to do things together both on and off campus. Hot Wells was a place where Vinnie could really belong.

Hot Wells High was only one of the many benefits of the San Antonio area for Vinnie, Frankie, and Doreen. The place was a virtual playground with lots to do and lots of sun to do it under. Vinnie and Doreen (Frankie was limited in his activities by his heart ailment) were everywhere, riding the buses and exploring the town. All three children were excellent swimmers and there were opportunities aplenty for swimming. In addition to the public swimming pools, they enjoyed swimming in the San Antonio River where they dove into the water from large overhanging trees. The pool at Brackenridge Park was another favorite. One afternoon while at the park, Vinnie noticed a young boy struggling in the water. Bobby Blunt, an eleven-year-old attending a church picnic, was drowning. Vinnie dove in, pulling the unconscious boy to safety. The fire department arrived and began resuscitation efforts. After ten nervous minutes, Bobby regained consciousness. Seeing the boy was going to be okay, Vinnie started to leave, but before he did someone took his picture. The next edition of the newspaper featured Vinnie's picture under a headline that read "Hero." Below the photograph was the story of his rescue of Bobby Blunt. Aside from his immediate family, Vinnie never bothered to mention this event to anyone.

Everything seemed to be better in Texas, even the home life. Confident that they were at last establishing roots as indicated by the purchase of the family's new home, the three kids began to make friends in earnest. Those friends were welcome in the Bates's home. The new house was located about fifteen miles from the high school, near the settlement of Elmendorf. Grover was still gone from time to time, but Clara was always at home. The family took meals together regularly and Clara was a good cook. They even had a dog, an Irish setter. They had all completely embraced family life and genuinely enjoyed each other's company. Laughs were plentiful and Clara was often in the middle of the fun, sometimes at her expense. Vinnie and Frankie were given to calling her "beaky" in reference to her slightly pronounced nose. Grover kidded her too—his nickname for her was "Gracie" for Gracie Allen's goofy persona in the Burns and Allen comedy team. That name stuck and soon everyone referred to her as Gracie. She never seemed to mind. The prior periods of family separation had been difficult for all involved, but any residual hard feelings were quickly fading.

The Flim Flam Man

Private detective W. H. Williams of Oklahoma City had been on a case of stolen firearms and ammunition for several months. The theft had occurred at an Oklahoma City hardware store and involved the loss of $10,000 in merchandise, a huge sum at the time. Williams's investigation traced the missing arms south to Texas. He believed the guns had been transferred to a smuggling syndicate which was transporting stolen goods into Mexico. Williams contacted local law enforcement officials in San Antonio and informed them of his progress in the case. The detective's investigative work was strong and persuasive, particularly his knowledge of the current whereabouts of the perpetrators and the location of their clearing house. The local police welcomed the news; someone else's legwork resulted in their credit for an arrest. On October 22, 1938, a swift noon raid was conducted by three deputies of the Bexar County Sheriff's Department with W. H. Williams in tow. The raid took place at a great stone house overlooking the San Antonio River near Elmendorf. It was the home of Grover and Clara Bates. Inside, officials seized seventeen rifles and four handguns. All the weapons were traceable to the Oklahoma City theft. At the house were Grover J. Bates and his brother Ray Bates. They were taken to the Bexar County jail for questioning.

The next day's papers, both the *San Antonio Light* and *San Antonio Express*, covered the story. It was big news. The stories told of a smashed smuggling syndicate and an arms and ammunition theft totaling, in this early report, more than $100,000. Police sources said the arms seized were only a portion of the total theft and that more guns may have been stashed in the area or already smuggled into Mexico. The *San Antonio Light* carried a photograph of the Bates brothers. The photograph was an interesting study in the demeanor of the accused men. Ray Bates appeared grim. His eyebrows were knitted; his mouth was stretched taunt, with lips slightly down-turned at the sides. He was slouching. His clothes are rumpled, his hair uncombed. In contrast to Ray's disheveled appearance, Grover was immaculate. Dressed in a dark suit, a white shirt and tie, he was well groomed with not a hair out of place. He sat upright but not rigid. His head was slightly upturned, his face open and bright. He looked confident. In short, Ray Bates looked like an accused thug and Grover, his lawyer.

The newspaper coverage did not end there. Two days later, news broke that Grover was also a fugitive from Vancouver, British Columbia, wanted in connection with swindling allegations amounting to $80,000. Grover's Canada problems stemmed from September, 1935 charges. Authorities in California had questions for Grover too. He was held without bail, an obvious flight risk. Due to the interstate and international aspects of the cases, Federal authorities were brought in. The State Department got involved, as their approval was required to extradite Grover to Canada. The unfolding newspaper stories also listed assumed names that Grover used: George Mason, Fred Sommers, F. H. Stout, Grover Burgess, E. A. Drennan, and Grover Clark. He exploited another name too. Ironically, after Grover had changed all of the step-children's surnames to Somers, he adopted theirs in his illegal activities when he called himself Grover Hume. News from British Columbia continued to flow south. Grover and two confederates, Thomas B. Jackson, alias Thomas Wilson, and Leo J. Drury,

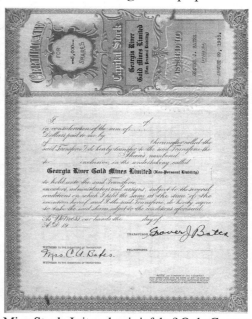

Mine Stock. Is it real or is it fake? Only Grover knows for sure. (*Starkey family collection*)

formed a team of confidence men running short and long "cons" to defraud victims by means of the "lost wallet trick" and also through a race horse betting scheme, among other ruses. The "bunco games" ran from 1930 to 1935. Due to the nature of the confidence schemes, most victims were reluctant to come forward and confess their own gullibility or greed. It was, after all, embarrassing to have allowed oneself to be cheated. The crimes for which Grover *could* be charged were two separate swindles committed against Spencer Pearse and A. C. Cadieu, both of Vancouver, British Columbia. These men were willing to testify. The amount associated with these two crimes totaled $13,848.

Canadian authorities wanted Grover to face justice for his crimes, but Grover was determined not to leave the States without a fight. He obtained the services of the law offices of Houston & Miskovsky of Oklahoma City in fighting extradition. United States Attorney W. R. Smith Jr. represented the interests of the Province of British Columbia. Grover's attorney successfully dragged the proceedings on for the next nine months while Grover remained in the custody of the U.S. Marshal in San Antonio. Finally, with his legal options exhausted, Grover was returned to Canada to face charges. For the crimes against Pearse and Cadieu, Grover pled guilty. He was sentenced to eighteen months hard labor for each crime, with the sentences to run concurrently. The duration of the sentence was considered to be light punishment. Grover did his time at the Oakalla Prison Farm in British Columbia.

The family's finances and emotions were completely drained after a nine month legal battle, and now they had to somehow carry on until Grover's return from prison. From this devastating situation, at least Vinnie gained understanding. He now understood why the family was always on the move and the reason for the children's name change; it was all done to avoid detection by law enforcement personnel. He understood why he and his siblings had been placed in so many different locales so often; his step-father had to travel fast and light to elude authorities and conduct business. Grover's self-professed traveling sales business had new meaning too. In retrospect, Vinnie could see that there was no better ruse than the role of a traveling salesman to give a fugitive a plausible excuse for being on the move. The boy now understood how the family was able to acquire a fancy house on the strength of traveling salesman's commissions. Vinnie learned it all by reading the newspapers. The period of domestic stability had been short-lived.

The Unsinkable Vinnie

Despite the shame and distraction of Grover's crimes, ongoing legal battles, and the ensuing high profile media coverage, Vinnie continued with his fun-loving, charismatic lifestyle largely unabated. If anything, he turned it up a notch. The freewheeling Vinnie was a force of fun to be reckoned with;

(San Antonio Light, San Antonio Express)

nowhere was there a better time than by his side. His youthful high-jinks were the stuff of Hot Wells High legend.

Once, Vinnie and his buddies were driving in an open car behind a heavily loaded slow-moving watermelon truck which was experiencing difficulty pulling a steep grade. Vinnie had an idea. He instructed the boy driving to pull near the back of the truck. Then Vinnie exited his passenger seat and moved along the hood to the point where he could leap from the car to the truck. Once on board the truck, he tossed watermelons to his companions, reentering the car before the vehicles crested the hill.

Another time, Vinnie, another boy and two girls, decided to make the trip to Landa Park in New Braunfels, Texas. Among Landa Park's attractions was a lake with boat rentals. The kids took Vinnie's Model A, arriving at dusk, after closing time. All were disappointed they had made the long trip for nothing. The boys thought there would be no harm in going into the park despite its closure. Gaining entry, they found the park rowboats neatly secured along the shoreline, but lacking oars. Vinnie had the solution. He found a discarded wooden packing crate which

35

he dismantled to use the slats as paddles. The four teens then went boating, paddling around the lake, and even stopping for an impromptu swim, fully-clothed. Eventually they returned to the boat dock and secured the boat in its proper location. Upon returning to the parking lot, they were met by police on patrol. The officers inquired if any of the kids had been in the park or in the water. Standing in soaking clothes that formed small puddles at their feet, the friends denied everything. Why, after all, the park was closed, wasn't it? The police surveyed the situation, saw that no damage had been done, and let them go. But

Vinnie, all dressed-up with lots of places to go. (*Hume family collection*)

that was only part of the adventure. On the way home, the Model A got a flat tire and Vinnie had no spare. The group debated a number of possible solutions. Finding none viable, Vinnie told everyone to pile back into the car—he would simply drive back home slowly on the grassy shoulder of the road in hopes the tire and wheel could withstand the trip. This they did. While the other teens nervously tried to monitor the tire's wear against their progress, Vinnie drove on without a care. He was still having a good time.

For Vinnie, the dating scene was wide-open. He dated many girls, and felt no allegiance to any one in particular. The dating was pretty tame, often in a group setting; double dating was the norm. All the same, he was something of a ladies' man, displaying his typical boldness and zeal around the fairer sex, without the usual self-consciousness of youth. Girls liked him instantly. He was a charmer. On one occasion, he met a new girl, asked her for a date, and she accepted. It was to be a double date, and Vinnie wheeled around and picked up the other couple first. That's when he confessed his dilemma. He had forgotten the girl's name and, worse, had lost her address. He thought he might remember the street name, so off the three went with Vinnie explaining along the way that he would knock on every door on both sides of the streets until he found her. The name part would be tough, he admitted, but he was sure he could get *her* to say it. If nothing else, his dating partners could immediately introduce themselves, thereby eliciting her name. Once on the street where he thought she lived, Vinnie began knocking on doors. He went to door after door with no success, as the couple in the back seat looked on in amusement. He wouldn't quit—he was making a full effort, but it was starting to get late and there was no end to the search in sight. Any longer and they would have to call the whole evening off. Finally, the couple saw Vinnie knock on a door that was answered by a pretty girl. Unfortunately, she was not the right one. But Vinnie stood there talking anyway. He talked for quite awhile. To the surprise of the other couple, the pretty girl, whom Vinnie had just met, got her coat and came along as his date. Everyone was amazed—except Vinnie. He just smiled that smile which closed his eyes to slits.

Out and about. Vinnie at the wheel, Doreen in the back seat at left. Frankie is seated on the fender at far right. (*Hume family collection*)

Back in school, Vinnie was involved in just about everything. He played tennis for Hot Wells, earning a letter in the sport. He wrote for the school newspaper, *The Echo*. He took part in school-wide activities such as "Kids' Day," a dress up day where the young adults donned clothing to make them appear as children. In keeping with his mischievous demeanor, Vinnie came to school on Kids' Day dressed only in a cloth diaper. He sported a bare chest and bare legs, with no apparent underwear beneath the diaper. That created a bit of a stir—enough that Principal Connell interceded and asked Vinnie to go home and get dressed. The teaching staff kept an eye on Vinnie for such shenanigans. He was always up to something, but nothing that amounted to a disciplinary problem. In fact, on more than one occasion while he was being reprimanded for his latest misdeed, a smile crept over the teacher's face. The disciplinarian would quickly send him away before smiling or laughing outright, which would have only reinforced Vinnie's behavior. In all, the teachers liked him and saw in him a very bright student who should have better applied himself to his studies. They counted on him too. The staff knew if Vinnie was part of a school production, not only would he arrive for practice prepared, but he would also be available to help others who were less prepared. Hot Wells staged an annual production featuring songs, skits, and dances. One such show was the *Hot*

The Russian Handkerchief Dance. Sister Doreen and Vinnie. (*Starkey family collection*)

Wells Air Castles of 1940, in which Vinnie demonstrated his expertise in dance. He was the best male dancer in the school, and his sister Doreen was the best female dancer. The siblings were paired for a dramatic Russian Handkerchief Dance, with Doreen portraying the character of Sonja and Vinnie as Petrov, dancing against the musical background of a gypsy band. It was the highlight of the costume production. When the show's run ended, the dancing didn't. Vinnie, Doreen, and their classmates formed a dance troupe that performed exhibitions for various service groups. They also presented a program at a nearby military base. These shows featured dancing to Texas swing music and were always well received.

Hot Wells was a small school where everybody knew everybody. The social circles mixed easily, but Vinnie was closest to a small group of friends that included Maude Walker, Jimmy Smith, Geraldine Helm, Jack Humphries, Stella McCarver, and Elgin Ernst. This group hung out together in the evenings at a place they called The Slough, on the banks of Salado Creek. They often walked along the shore, sometimes building a campfire, or sitting around in an old abandoned cabin to talk. Sometimes the boys drank beer.

At the Slough. Frankie front row far left, Vinnie front row far right. (*Wilmer Duderstadt*)

Vinnie's years at Hot Wells High were his happiest so far, offering him a wide range of diversions in his personal and social life. These diversions did not distract him from his relationship with his brother and sister, however. Vinnie was close to and protective of his sister Doreen. Vinnie and Doreen were both close and attentive to the sickly Frankie. Frankie loved them both. The bond they had all forged during the family's nomadic period remained strong.

Hot Wells High's graduating class of 1940 was the school's first to attend through 12th grade. Previously, those wishing to continue their education in the 12th grade had to attend elsewhere, as those level classes were not offered at Hot Wells. That first full commencement ceremony saw the graduation of thirty-two students, among them Vinnie Somers who, like so many other graduates, was poised to make his own way in the world.

The Hot Wells Class of 1940. Vinnie in the front row, far right. (*Hume family collection*)

A False Start

Vinnie's future was delayed. Grover had not yet been released from the Canadian penitentiary, and the family needed the financial support of Vinnie, its eldest male. They had already moved to lower monthly expenses, but without Vinnie's help they couldn't manage. So Vinnie's part-time job as a service attendant at Kalite Oil Company, a gas station on South Pressa Street, became a full-time position. The money he would have saved toward college was used to cover the family's living expenses. After years of being dropped off here and there all around the country waiting for Grover to return, Vinnie was back in the same old situation—waiting for Grover to return to pick up his responsibilities. It must have seemed that Grover and Vinnie were both in a prison of Grover's making. Still Vinnie did not complain. He did what he knew he had to do. He wouldn't give Frankie and Doreen the impression that it was their fault he had to put his plans on hold.

The teaching staff at Hot Wells High School, noting that Vinnie was not attending college, asked if he might consider helping out with some of the school's extracurricular activities on a volunteer basis. He agreed and was promptly made editor-in-chief of *The Echo* newspaper. In addition to his editing duties, Vinnie covered school sporting events as a reporter. He also served as the manager for The Esquires, the school's swing band. The following spring he was offered yet another volunteer opportunity, this time as the assistant producer and performer in the presentation of *Hot Wells Air Castles of 1941*. The 1941 show was performed in two segments. The first half featured fast moving vaudeville-style acts, while the second was a musical version of Hansel and Gretel. Vinnie and Doreen performed dance routines throughout the program and, as in the previous year, were showcased as a duo. The response to the show was very positive. Vinnie signed off his year of volunteerism at Hot Wells High School with a stirring editorial in *The Echo* recapping the success of the school's academic, social, and sporting year.

College Bound

At last, Vinnie, upon Grover's return, was on his way to college. He would attend Sam Houston State College in Huntsville, Texas. His educational pursuits would be in the field of medicine, a career choice, he said, that was motivated by his brother's protracted illness. But it is likely that there were other motivating factors as well.

Where Do They Come From?

For many individuals, Vinnie included, it didn't seem that they chose to become doctors, but rather that the medical profession chose them. A surprising number of doctors were raised in emotionally handicapped families where parental involvement was limited. Inadequate parental connections may have resulted from any number of personal issues including addiction, absenteeism, or emotional disorder. Whatever the reason, children from such families, particularly the eldest, customarily assumed the role of caregiver to younger members of the family, and sometimes to the parents as well. These young caregivers, who later entered the medical profession, shared a number of other traits stemming from their family backgrounds. Feeling little in the way of parental support and approval, they were conditioned to quest for perfectionism and academic overachievement, all in an effort to buoy self-esteem. These powerful behaviors in caregiving and academic overachievement proved very useful in attaining their goal of becoming medical doctors. Upon reaching the position of doctor, and with it societal admiration and affirmation, other needs relating to childhood would be met and maintained, especially for those, like Vinnie, with the needs of a narcissist.

The Narcissist

In Greek mythology, a boy caused the death of Echo by rejecting her love. In response to the girl's death, the goddess of retributive justice, Nemesis, punished the boy by causing him to fall in love with his own image as reflected in a pool of water. The boy died there longing for himself, in much the same way Echo had died yearning for him. The boy's name was Narcissus and the mythological tale of his demise would come to serve as the namesake for and representation of a personality disorder associated with matters of self-image.

Popular culture's characterization of a narcissist is of an individual with a greatly inflated sense of self-love. Such a definition is, at the least, incomplete. Rather than self-love, the narcissist loves his *reflection*. Social standing, celebrity, or title may be the foundation of that reflection, but any recognition, adoration, or status reflected from other persons is the type of validation the narcissist needs, seeks, and comes to expect.

The cause of narcissistic behavior is thought to be environmental, its genesis in childhood emotional development. It is the effect of inconsistent acceptance by parents and other close authority figures which gives way to feelings of inadequacy and eventual fears of abandonment. Narcissism may therefore be viewed as an adaptive strategy allowing the individual a "false self," one worthy of respect while the "true self" plays a far lesser role. The narcissist's true self is not lost altogether, it is simply that he prefers the image.

Seemingly contrary to public perceptions of this behavior

is the lack of selfishness intrinsic in the narcissist's true self. Because reflected self-image is essential to the narcissist, he often puts his own real needs last, in a tireless effort to keep his image alive and vital. It is an effort typified by overwork, chance-taking, or other larger than life behaviors. It's usually a public performance designed to elicit adulation.

Certain professions provide a "safe harbor" for persons with narcissistic traits. Among them are politics, corporate management, and the medical profession.

Huntsville

Founded in 1879 in Huntsville, Texas, Sam Houston State Teacher's College, by the time of Vinnie's arrival in the fall of 1941, was an older, well-established state run facility for the education and training of teachers. It was a fine school for general basic higher education too; a place where prerequisites for programs offered elsewhere could be obtained. The campus grounds were highlighted by large pine trees and manicured lawns. Three large dormitories and as many residence halls offered home-style living. The campus buildings were of brick construction, the oldest buff-colored, the newer buildings red. Six buildings held classrooms. The campus also had a music building, a band hall, and a large sports stadium. The student body numbered approximately 1,100—huge when compared to Hot Wells. It was a co-ed college, but the female population far outnumbered the males.

Student life was casual and friendly. It wasn't a big party school, as Huntsville was a dry town. Alcoholic beverages were available in the surrounding counties, but one had to secure transportation and money to obtain them—a combination, for college students, that was in short supply.

Once a month, Ed Gerlach's orchestra "The Houstonians" performed big band music at the campus field house, an extremely popular event that drew huge crowds of both students and non-students.

When Vinnie began the fall semester at Sam Houston, he was joined by Hot Wells alumni Maude Walker and Jimmy Smith. Vinnie and Jimmy paired up as roommates at Midge's Boarding House just off campus, near the school. It was a small house with rooms for six boys, but about twenty students were fed there. Because Midge's meals were renowned for being the best home-style food around, there was a waiting list to get a meal ticket. The boarding house had a large front porch where the boys lounged around on warm evenings.

Vinnie and Jimmy partnered on the purchase of a Ford Model

A Roadster. They festooned the car with a foxtail attached to the radiator cap and reflectors that were all the rage at the time. The two friends got along well as roommates. Jimmy, attending Sam Houston on an athletic scholarship, was often gone on road trips. When Jimmy returned, he was always pleased to see that Vinnie had posted his assignments on a board in their room. Both boys, along with two other friends, attended Sun-

Vinnie and the Model A Ford. (*Hume family collection*)

day church services regularly. Because each was of a different faith, they chose to attend services on a rotating basis, Methodist, · Presbyterian, Baptist and, for Vinnie's turn, Catholic.

On weekends the two boys sometimes made the nearly ten-hour round trip from school to San Antonio and back again. The trips were often an adventure. On one occasion as they were returning to the Huntsville campus, they encountered a violent windstorm. A freezing cold north wind hit Vinnie and Jimmy with full force as they motored onward without the benefit of a heater in the unprotected topless car. The cold was unbearable. Finally, they pulled over and searched the car for anything that might provide a shelter against the wind. They found an Army blanket. Then they tore away some of the already loose floorboard slats to expose the exhaust manifold to the passenger area of the car. Unfolding the blanket, they sat on one end pulling the fabric across their backs and up over their heads. Jimmy gripped the blanket with both hands and held it to the windshield frame. Vinnie also held the blanket to the windshield frame with one hand, while using the other to steer the car. The trip resumed, and the boys—now exposed to the engine heat and with their "blanket top" in place—were able to hold hypothermia at bay long enough to reach Huntsville. On another trip back to school, Vinnie and Jimmy were tired, cold, and hungry on the edge of the town of Schulenburg. They decided to stop at a café in hopes someone would take pity on a pair of poor starving college kids and buy them a cup of coffee and a donut—something folks did for college kids in those days. The café was quite full, so the two found themselves walking all the way to the back to find a seat. There, sitting in the back was a deputy sheriff, a law officer with the reputation of being rough and free with his ticket writing. The boys knew him and were afraid of him. They knew something else about him too. The married deputy had a tendency to dally with other women. When his firecracker of a wife learned of these flings, she was known to physically attack him, inflicting pain. And there he sat in the back of the café, but he was not alone. The sheriff caught sight of Vinnie and Jimmy, recognizing them both. Soon the boys were treated to all the coffee and donuts they could eat, all compliments of the deputy sheriff.

Eventually, Vinnie traded in the Model A for a Mercury convertible. He didn't bother to consult his roommate on the transaction, despite Jimmy's half ownership. In fact, the first Jimmy learned of the new acquisition was when he saw Vinnie driving around in the Merc. It surprised Jimmy a little but he trusted his friend and, sure enough, when the boys later went their separate ways, Jimmy was reimbursed for his half of the car.

The car, their social lives, and even their educations seemed trivial in proportion to the information the boys received at a Sunday night church service, or Vespers as it was called. The service was late in starting. A half-hour passed without so much as an explanation for the delay. Finally the college president and four faculty members addressed those assembled and reported the news of the day. It was December 7, 1941. Japan had bombed Pearl Harbor. The students were shocked, each struggling for the meaning of the event and how it would affect the world and their lives. Jimmy's most immediate concern was for his brother, Joe, stationed aboard the battleship Oklahoma at Pearl Harbor. Vinnie may have wondered about his role in the defense of the United States, for he was still a Canadian citizen, and was still using an alias his step-father had assigned him. All that was soon to change.

Day is Done

Vinnie carried a heavy class load into the New Year at Sam Houston while ever-mindful of the war in the Pacific. He was troubled as well by the struggle his younger brother was experiencing at home. Frankie's fragile health worsened.

Frankie's attendance at Hot Wells had always been irregular because of his health. He continued his education through a mix of classroom and home studies, spending the majority of the time at home. His fellow students at the high school, however, still had ample opportunity to get to know the brother of the popular Vinnie and Doreen. Frankie was accepted on his own merits as a sweet, likable kid. He participated in school events to the extent his health allowed, even joining the football team. His involvement was more as an honorary teammate, but a teammate just the same. Frankie was treated as a bona fide member of the student body, and he longed to make a greater contribution to student life. He enlisted his biological father, John Hume, in that regard. He wrote his father asking if John might locate a music store that carried bagpipe lessons, as Frankie was aware that the Scotch Lassie Pep Club had bagpipes and an interested player, but was unable to obtain instructional materials. Perhaps it wasn't much, but Frankie wanted to help in any way he could.

The students wanted to help Frankie too. In times of meager personal finances, the students raised money to purchase him tokens of their affection: a pair of red and white striped silk pajamas and a plant for his bedroom.

A persisting period of almost complete bed rest began in February of 1942. Frankie, though bedridden, was cheerful and talkative. He kept up with his schoolwork as well. Gracie, the absent mother on so many past occasions, was absent no more, tirelessly caring for her youngest son with good cheer and without complaint.

Vinnie returned from college and during the summer break went to work at Southern Steel, a manufacturer of prison chambers. It was hard work under the hot San Antonio sun, carrying and riveting the heavy steel jail bars and doors for construction of cells for the Texas state penal system. When off work, Vinnie spent a lot of time with his brother. With his job earnings he bought Frankie an automobile. It wasn't much of a car, but it was Frankie's, and Vinnie parked it right outside his ailing brother's bedroom window so Frankie could look upon it and dream of the good times to come in a car of his very own. As summer moved into fall, Vinnie took a job with Keenan, Searles & Sullivan, downtown at the ornate National Bank of Commerce professional building. Vinnie decided he would forego the upcoming school year at Sam Houston, believing he and the income he provided, even with Grover's return, were needed at home. Also, he was still considering entering the military.

Throughout the winter of 1942 and the next spring, Frankie's physical condition continued to deteriorate, but he was still making big plans. He talked of all the things he would do in the car Vinnie bought him, and he planned a trip to Canada to see his father. Frankie didn't know he was dying. Everyone else did. Friends and family tried to keep up his spirits. Bacterial endocarditis in conjunction with the heart valve defects was shortening his life. Doreen and a friend, both nursing students, often cared for Frankie, offering Gracie some relief from her constant caregiving.

Near the end, Gracie was so exhausted and distressed that a nurse sedated her. She was sleeping when Frankie passed away. When she woke, Grover, overwrought with grief and sobbing, was unable to tell his wife the news; instead Doreen told her that Frankie was dead. It was April 22, 1943. He was nineteen years old. Two days later, funeral services were held at the chapel of the Alamo Funeral Home. Because he was to be laid to rest in a non-Catholic graveyard, a priest refused to conduct the service. Instead, a Baptist minister performed the service to a full chapel. Gracie was pleased to see her son had so many friends and so many people sent flowers. The boy was interred at Mission Burial Park. Gracie wrote her ex-husband John a three-page letter thanking him for his significant cash contribution which helped cover burial expenses. She also wrote John of the tenderness of their son's soul, and how she was sure he was in heaven. She reported on the beauty of the well-attended funeral. She wrote that she had taken care of Frankie very well and that their son had never suffered a single bedsore. She wasn't taking credit for her caregiving; she was clearly trying to comfort John in his grief. Gracie knew grief. She was completely devastated with her son's passing. She experienced incapacitating headaches and a persistent melancholy. Eventually, she had an emotional breakdown. In an effort to break free of her deep depression, Gracie agreed to submit to electroconvulsive therapy, commonly known as electric shock treatment. The procedure, conducted over several sessions, seemed to help Gracie recover. The grief associated with Frankie's passing did not disappear entirely, for Gracie or any of the family, but with time it became manageable.

The New American

Vinnie's sense of loss was acute as well. He was able to combat it, in part, by undertaking several life changes. The first

Serving his new country. (*Hume family collection*)

happened before Frankie's passing when Vinnie officially changed his name from Vincent Hume to Vincent Somers in March of 1943. He had used the alias Grover had given him for so long that it seemed more his name than his birth name, so he made it legal. He applied for U.S. citizenship and, with the application on file, he enlisted in the United States Army.

His military induction was at Fort

Sam Houston Receiving Center. From there he was sent to Camp Joseph T. Robinson, located north of Little Rock, Arkansas, where he underwent basic training. While there, his citizenship application was approved and he was sworn in as a U.S. citizen in Little Rock, on June 21, 1943. Vinnie's ambition, even prior to enlistment, was to fly in the Army Air Corps. Pilot hopefuls were required to pass a written examination. Vinnie knew that his old college roommate Jimmy Smith had taken and passed the entrance exam to the aviation cadet program, so he called Jimmy and asked about the test. The two met and Jimmy helped Vinnie study for the lengthy exam. Vinnie took the test and passed it, but was disqualified for medical reasons as a result of a pre-existing ear condition. This was a great disappointment. Meanwhile, Vinnie and his fellow soldiers of C Company were deployed in domestic service in rescue and relief efforts associated with the devastating Missouri, Arkansas, and Mississippi River floods of 1943 which caused more than $100 million in property losses. During a period of down time, the soldiers were offered a volunteer opportunity involving the testing of a piece of experimental equipment. Vinnie was chosen from among the volunteers and underwent the test, which left him with additional and substantial hearing damage, enough so that by October he was issued an Honorable Discharge by reason of physical disability.

Work and School

Vinnie's return to the civilian world gave him two options: find a job or return to school. He chose both. He found employment at San Antonio's Kelly Field and enrolled in St. Mary's University.

St. Mary's, founded in 1852, was a private, Catholic, co-educational school. Situated on a huge sprawling campus, the school was located only minutes from downtown San Antonio. The campus buildings were a mix of modern and classic structures. It had the look of an upscale institution. St. Mary's boasted a low student-to-teacher ratio, helping ensure a quality higher education experience. Certainly it was a fine place to earn a first rate education, but it was expensive compared to a state college. Vinnie was working while attending school, but it was still not enough. To make ends meet, he needed financial help, which he received from his father John.

Along the way, Vinnie met a girl. She was a nursing school friend of Doreen's named Beverly Walker. Beverly saw in Vinnie a fun-loving young man with a zany sense of humor. Their frequent date of choice was to go dancing. The two saw each other for several years and even spoke of marriage, but not seriously. Vinnie wasn't in the habit of speaking too seriously about anything.

The next year found Vinnie back at St. Mary's, but with new places of employment. He worked two part-time jobs—at Trinity Pharmacy and the Alamo Funeral Home. For the funeral home he drove an ambulance, on call at all hours. One night, speeding to an accident scene, he too had an accident. Cresting a hill, he found a herd of sheep blocking the highway. Attempting to take evasive action, Vinnie lost control of the ambulance and rolled it, killing a large number of the animals but luckily escaped injury himself. This mishap with a vehicle was the first of many.

After completing a second year of college at St. Mary's, Vinnie, still intent on pursuing a medical degree, took the entrance examination for Baylor University College of Medicine.

4

The Lady and the Doctor

Trouble Brewing

Originally a great medical complex was to be built in Dallas, Texas, by the Southwestern Medical Foundation. The Foundation approached the trustees of Baylor University with an offer to have the school's prestigious medical college, also located in Dallas, made a part of the new facility. The offer had its merits. On land provided by the Foundation, a new modern school of medicine and dentistry would be constructed. Along with the new buildings, new equipment would be purchased and installed. Ongoing financial support was offered as well. The deal meant progress and growth for the school. It also came with substantial conditions. In exchange for growth and progress, Baylor would relinquish most its control over the medical school. The promised land and buildings were to forever remain under the ownership of the Foundation. The administrative committee, established under the deal to govern the school, was to be comprised of three members installed by the Foundation and two from the trustees of Baylor. In a split and uneasy decision, the trustees accepted the offer. Some of the trustees adopted a wait-and-see attitude to how the deal would play out—there would still be time to opt out in the future if untenable conditions arose. Those conditions were quickly presented.

The Foundation entered into another agreement with the City of Dallas for the use of Parkland Hospital as a clinical facility under a provision that the medical college be entirely free of religious involvement. This placed Baylor University, with its Baptist influence, in a position without a voice, to be totally absorbed by the Foundation. The only remaining option to Baylor University was to cancel the agreement with the Foundation. Feeling that their hands had been forced by the Foundation's agreement with the city, the Baylor trustees voted to terminate the agreement. They also decided to look for a new home for the school, somewhere outside of Dallas, an action that was met with much criticism from within the Dallas medical community. The Southwestern Medical Foundation made plans to establish its own college of medicine. Hard feelings abounded. Media relations soured. To the school's trustees, it was evident that Baylor University was not being allowed to leave; it was being forced out.

Houston

After forty-three years, Dallas would no longer be home to Baylor University. Inquiries with the M.D. Anderson Foundation in Houston were showing promise for a move to that city. The M.D. Anderson Foundation had a medical center of its own in the planning stages and Baylor University would fit perfectly into the plan.

An offer was made that included a site for the college, $1,000,000 in construction funding, and an additional $1,000,000 in research funding payable in $100,000 annual installments. The Anderson Foundation would have no part in the operation of the college. The community of Houston rallied around the deal with the Chamber of Commerce pledging annual payments of $50,000 for a ten-year period to aid in the school's operating expenses. Area hospitals readily agreed to affiliate with the school of medicine. Houston clearly wanted Baylor. The school's trustees accepted the offer. Now they faced the overwhelming task of moving before the start of the school's next session, to a location in Houston that had yet to be determined. With building construction still years off (these were the war years when building materials and manpower were in short supply) a temporary facility had to be obtained. Finally a building was found and leased. It was a two story brick and stone building with a basement located at Buffalo Drive and Lincoln Street. It had last been a Sears, Roebuck & Company retail store. With a light remodeling effort, and the move from Dallas complete, it was ready for use. The school's next scheduled period of instruction for 1943-44 had been met. That first session in Houston was completed in March of 1944 with commencement ceremonies for sixteen graduates.

Baylor University in the Sears-Roebuck building. (*A History of Baylor University College of Medicine 1900-1953*)

Vince Goes to Baylor

Baylor admission requirements were relaxed during the war years in an attempt to accelerate the process of bringing much-needed new doctors into practice. Instead of the ninety semester hours of undergraduate work previously required for admission, Vince needed seventy-two. His freshman year at Baylor began on September 3, 1945. Classes were still being conducted in the rather humble environment of the old Sears building, but plans were progressing for the construction of the new Baylor. About 100 acres of property had been recently purchased from the City of Houston in what was Hermann Park. Vince and his fellow students knew that one day they would attend the new school, but their education for the immediate future would be confined to the old Sears building. The main floor contained the library, classrooms, and the anatomy lab. The upstairs housed a few more classrooms. Dogs, used for medical experiments, were kenneled in the basement, the only air-conditioned area. The building contained little in the way of aesthetics or even permanency. The interior walls were loose, unpainted, and thin. Sometimes lectures could be overheard from nearby rooms. But while the setting was temporary, the education was built to last. This was a first-rate school of medicine, and the students, sometimes a little cocky with the headiness of it all, were ever-mindful of the tremendous opportunity before them. Idealism ran high.

Vince's first year at Baylor involved studies in the basic medical sciences. Classes included Histology, the study of microscopic anatomy; Comparative Anatomy, as the name suggests the study of the similarities and differences in the structure of living organisms; the difficult Biochemistry, parts biology and chemistry focusing on the substances found in living organisms; Physiology, studies of living cells, tissues and organs sometimes referred to as functional anatomy; and also Anatomy. At Baylor, Anatomy was often referred to as the "weed-out class" due to the degree of difficulty in the material and because of the lab work. The class was taught by the highly respected and well-liked John Haley, M.D. Much of the lab work concerned the dissection of human cadavers, a difficult experience for some new students. The cadavers came primarily from two sources. As a provision of their wills, people had donated their bodies to science. Other cadavers were provided by cities which had held unidentified bodies for a year or more. The lab work was performed by a group of four students on a cadaver with each student taking turns performing, assisting, or observing the dissection. Initially the students, most of whom had never seen a dead body, were a bit hesitant in their work. But any feeling of apprehension quickly disappeared when they realized this was why they had come—this was how medicine was learned.

An eight-hour school day of intensive instruction was tough, followed by an equally daunting test of self-discipline: four to five hours of after-school study. The Baylor professors, aware of the tremendous academic commitment made by their students, openly showed support and encouragement in appreciation of that dedication. Other avenues of support were available to the students of Baylor. Some found assistance and friendship by joining a fraternity.

The Frat Brother

Vince joined the Phi Chi Fraternity and, as was common for freshmen, roomed at the frat house on Lovett Boulevard. The home was in a pleasant, though aging, part of town. The fraternity house was a large two story tan brick structure with a tile roof. From the frat house it was a twenty minute walk to the school. The house was home to twenty-five members of the fraternity, mostly freshmen. It was a clean, orderly, and well-maintained residence with two maids and a cook. Frat brothers who stayed at nearby boarding houses stopped by the house to take meals and socialize.

Vince was a good fit in the fraternity—an outgoing, upbeat, and well-liked brother. He seemed to attract women which didn't hurt his popularity among his brothers.

He was always available and willing to take part in weekend sporting events the fraternity scheduled in competition with other Baylor organizations. Vince was involved in more than a few high-jinks as well. One weekend, as the brothers sat around the house playing cards, someone suggested that an alcoholic beverage might be in order. A quick perusal of the liquor cabinet revealed that while a great many bottles were on hand, they were of differing brands and blends, with no bottle containing a sufficient amount of liquor to mix drinks for everyone. After some spirited debate, it was decided that all the bottles, the whiskeys, bourbons, scotches, liqueurs and whatever else was available, would be mixed together to formulate a kind of Phi Chi "super drink." Understanding that such a concoction had a high potential for bad taste, all took an oath that they would drink the mixed beverage no matter the outcome. Plan in place, the next step was to locate a large mixing bowl. They could find none. The only alternative, someone suggested, was to use one of the bathtubs. And so they mixed the witch's brew in a frat house bathtub. Upon sampling the new libation, a few of the brothers even had the audacity to say that the mixture wasn't half bad.

Laughs, sporting events, and card playing were the order of relaxing weekends for Vince and his frat brothers. It was all about low cost activities designed to distract them from their overwhelming academic workload. Of course "relaxing weekend" was relative, especially when applied to a medical student. For Vince, a typical relaxing weekend meant studying until midnight on Friday evening, followed by Saturday studies that lasted until about noon. Perhaps then the remainder of Saturday was left for relaxation. Sunday meant church services and more relaxation, at least until Sunday evening when he returned to the books after dinner, studying late into the night. Somehow this schedule produced good results. Although not an academic standout—everyone enrolled at Baylor Medical was highly intelligent—Vince had little trouble with the work and was considered a bright and able student.

The Sophomore

For Vince and the other sixty-six sophomores entering Baylor in early September, 1946, the year's tuition was considered high at $480. Baylor's status as a first-rate private school had not been diminished, nor its tuition lowered, despite its modest rebirth in Houston. This transitional state was still very much evident in Vince's second year at the school, when it was back to the old Sears and Roebuck building again. But as before, the education was so dynamic, and the students and staff of the University so committed to the program that it didn't seem to matter.

Vince's basic medical science classes for his second year at Baylor were a mix of those that continued from his freshman year, such as Physiology, with the addition of new classes that included Pathology, a difficult and important class relating to the process and result of diseases; Pharmacology, the study of drugs and their effects; Embryology, a biology class focusing on the development of embryos and the growth of the fetus; Bacteriology, the study of bacteria and diseases associated with bacteria; and Neuroanatomy, concerning brain and nerve function. Second year lab work incorporated Physiological and Pharmacology studies with experiments on dogs. The students brought the canines up from their basement kennels and anesthetized them. Each dog was placed on a lab table for four students. The presiding professor provided step by step instructions for the ensuing procedures. It most cases, the students opened the abdomen, inspected the organs and their function, and viewed the reaction of the organs to the anesthesia. Specific organ reactions were recorded as were blood pressure and heart rate changes. Later, simple surgeries were performed on the dogs to give students experience working on living creatures. The experiments also helped students become accustomed to using surgical instruments, working while wearing gloves, and getting blood on their hands. At the conclusion of the experiments, the dogs were euthanized. More so than their freshmen year, the volume of material the students were given to learn bordered on overwhelming. The only way to succeed was to increase off campus study time.

Off Campus

In his sophomore year, Vince and several other classmates took up residence in a boarding house. The boarding house was primarily a place to sleep and study. Meals were still taken at the Phi Chi Fraternity House, which was also the center of social activity. Vince continued to participate in frat athletic contests, house parties, and games of bridge.

An interesting development occurred that year. Incoming freshmen were not subjected to the pledge hazing that Vince's class had endured. The hazing for Vince and his fellow pledges had been light, on the order of being blindfolded then driven around and dropped off in the middle of nowhere to find their way back to the frat house. But Vince's sophomore class demanded that even light hazing be discontinued. After all, they reasoned, wasn't medical school enough of an undertaking without the added anxiety? Hazing seemed, for all involved, a waste of time, humiliating and not much fun. The practice was stopped.

In his two years at Baylor, Vince had acquired a number of close friends in and outside the fraternity including Charlie Meadows, Dave Davis, and Californians Richard Sterkel and Keith White. Of the latter two, fellow students would say, "Vince could start a sentence, and Sterkel and White would finish it," so close was their friendship. When not hanging out at the frat house, Vince and his buddies frequented a number of their favorite spots, such as the soda fountain at Tower Drug or The Quality Sandwich Shop, where they talked and laughed while appraising Houston's female population. Early in 1947 while seated in a booth at The Quality Sandwich Shop, Vince and his pals noticed a booth full of girls. The girls noticed them back, but no connection was made. Later, as the girls were reliving that shared moment of observation, they discussed which of the guys they would like to date if the opportunity arose. In turn they each described their favorite young man. When it came to Myrtle Bush's turn, she said, "I want the cute one with the squinty eyes."

Myrt

A family could barely sustain life while sharecropping. It was farming at the lowest possible level, utterly lacking in hope for the future. By 1936, Bob and Pearl Bush had had enough of sharecropping. In an effort to make a new start, Bob, Pearl, and their seven children moved from Crosby, Texas to a small forty-acre farm of their own near Highland in Erath County, Texas. The acreage would produce enough food for the family to subsist on, but there would be little money for what, in a later time, would be termed as "necessities," but were then referred to as "extras." But what mattered most was that it was a place of their own, a place to build equity and a future. The farm had a four-bedroom wood frame house which Bob built with the help of a friend. The house was not served by electricity or by indoor plumbing. The farm's outbuildings consisted of a barn, a smokehouse, and a privy. A small orchard included plum, pecan, peach, and fig trees. For livestock there were milk cows, calves, chickens, and hogs. Teddy, the family dog, was the only non-producing animal.

The principal crops, in addition to those raised for their own consumption, were cotton, corn, and melons. All the children helped on the farm. It was brutally hot work. Working in the cotton fields was the worst of it. From the very planting, it was miserable stuff to be around. Cotton seeds could not be planted effectively by mechanical means because bits of lint attached to the seeds prevented even flow and distribution. The family used a mechanical planter, but the uneven sowing caused them the arduous task of thinning out unwanted plants. Throughout the growing cycle the seemingly unending process of weeding recurred. Harvest time was tremendously labor-intensive too. The plants reached approximately two feet in height, which forced the pickers to bend at the waist to pick the cotton. Cotton picking, removing a boll of fiber from its hard, sharp pointed hull, was tedious and often painful. The sharp points of the hull were frequently driven under the cuticles, causing bleeding and soreness in the fingertips, potentially leading to infection. The container used for collecting the cotton was a long tube-like sack, strapped across the neck and shoulder and dragged behind the picker as he or she moved between the rows. The harvest could linger beyond the main effort too. In a process called "scrapping," the family returned to the fields to collect cotton bolls from scattered plants that had not matured during the initial picking.

The fresh produce also required work, though it was less strenuous than raising cotton. An added benefit of raising produce was that it could be sold without passing through a middleman. On occasion the Bushes loaded up their Model A Ford truck and made the trip to the landing at Lynchburg to sell their farm fresh produce—honeydew and banana melons, cantaloupes, corn, tomatoes, and peppers—to travelers waiting for the ferry.

Life on the farm was hard work and still it wasn't enough to cover the family's living expenses. To make ends meet, Bob and Pearl worked both on and off the farm. Taking any employment he could find, Bob worked for the Works Progress Administration, logged, and served as a night watchman. During his time as a logger, he harvested holly and clover and brought it home to make into cloverine salve, which the family sold along the roadside. Bob made whiskey too, at a hidden still down by a creek, away from the eyes of revenuers. Pearl worked at a fig canning plant in Highland and was known to make a little wine. During those Depression years they did what they had to do, as all families did, to eke out a living. They were very poor. Sometimes it seemed like all they did, children included, was eat, work, and sleep. It was a hard life but it was made easier by the mutual affection and shared values of the family members. Education and regular church attendance were especially important. A standard of discipline and respect was observed. The Bushes got along well together, and even as a rift developed between Bob and Pearl—one that would eventually end the marriage—the children knew they were loved by both parents.

Myrtle had just finished the second grade when her family moved from Crosby, the place of her birth, to the larger nearby town of Highland. She grew tall and skinny, with a penchant for speaking her mind and taking action when necessary. Once, during fourth grade, Myrtle brought a length of rope to school to use to play double jump rope. A classmate, who happened to be the mayor's son, made the double mistake of trying to steal Myrtle's jump rope while making a malicious remark regarding her mother's Jewish heritage. Myrtle gave him a sound thrashing with the very rope he tried to steal. She received a scolding from the principal, missed the bus, and had to walk the two miles home. The consequences were worth it though; the mayor's son never bothered Myrtle again.

Myrtle, like her siblings, garnered a strong work ethic during her formative years on the farm. Besides tending crops and caring for livestock, there were a myriad of other domestic chores such as churning butter, making cottage cheese, and washing clothes on a rub board. The youngsters sometimes earned a little money for their labor. Bob paid them for the low-yield and time-consuming cotton scrapping. With their meager earnings, the children traded with the traveling salesmen whose circuits brought them to Highland twice a year. Having learned from her mother how to sew on a treadle machine, Myrtle sometimes purchased fabric and notions. She made doll clothing, gathered skirts, and proudly completed her first quilt top at the age of twelve. While Myrtle was still twelve years old, Bob and Pearl's marriage ended acrimoniously. The divorce played out in the courts with the children forced to take the witness stand. They were asked with which parent they wished to reside. Myrtle chose to stay on the farm with her father.

Bob Bush enjoyed being a father and he was a good one. His personality was generally serious, with a loving and sometimes demonstrative side when it came to his children. He believed in strong discipline, but did not spank. He was illiterate but wise, poor yet generous. His word was gold. He was a good man and Myrtle, whom he called "Baby," revered him. He was an easy person to respect. Even in the aftermath of a litigious divorce, he never spoke poorly of Pearl. At times that must have been difficult. When Myrtle badly injured her wrist during PE class in junior high, x-rays were required. With no cash on hand, Bob sold a calf to pay for the x-ray. Several days later, the police arrived at the farm and took Bob away. An upset Myrtle asked her father why he had to leave with the police.

Bob's response was simply, "They found out what a bad cook I am, Baby." Jailed overnight, Bob was home the next day. Again Myrtle asked why, and again Bob simply remarked that it was due to his poor cooking skills. It was years before Myrtle learned the truth. Pearl had turned her ex-husband in for the sale of the calf, claiming the animal was a designated part of her property settlement and that Bob had in effect stolen the calf and sold it. Bob never mentioned Pearl's involvement in the fiasco to the children, nor did he seem to dwell on the affair; there just wasn't time for such nonsense. Bob was right, there wasn't much time left.

In the early morning hours of January 8, 1944, Myrtle heard her father cry out for her brother Joe. Sensing urgency, and with Joe sleeping, Myrtle responded. She found her father in desperate need of medical attention. Myrtle woke Joe and told him to stay with their father while she went for help. It started to rain as she dashed barefoot onto the porch. Sprinting a half mile, she reached the closest neighbor and told them of the situation. The neighbor went directly to the farm while Myrtle ran on to the Dean family home, the closest neighbor with a telephone. It was 3 A.M. when she was finally able to make her distress call. Seven long hours later, the doctor arrived. Bob had suffered a massive stroke. He required hospitalization, but with little money he would have to go to a hospital for the poor. To get care at a charity hospital, Bob needed a recommendation, someone who could vouch for his poverty. The family's Baptist minister vouched for Bob, and an ambulance picked him up at 6 P.M. He didn't survive the night.

Her father's passing left Myrtle in mourning; the frightening events of his death left her traumatized. Her pain did not go quickly.

After Bob's death, Pearl moved back to the farm. Although she had been largely out of touch with the children who had chosen to live with her ex-husband, life for all resumed with relative normalcy. Pearl, despite a few annoying habits, such as relentless nagging and a near obsession regarding money, was not a bad person or mother. She loved her children and looked out for their interests. She had few qualms about standing up for them if she felt they were being treated unfairly in school or elsewhere.

For Pearl the farm was an asset and little more. She longed to return to Houston where she had resided since the divorce. So Pearl, with Myrtle's enthusiastic help, fixed up the farmhouse. Myrtle was not let in on the plan to sell the house; she thought the old house was being spruced up for the family's enjoyment. But with new exterior paint and interior wallpapering, the house and farm were put on the market and sold.

By her late teens, Myrtle, who preferred to be called Myrt, had grown into a tall, slim beauty. She was outgoing and laughed easily. She was no shrinking violet, owning a strong personality and willing to speak her mind. She had great female friends, but was quite comfortable in the company of men. In Houston, she found work in a variety of jobs. She worked as a clerk, first at Rettig's Ice Cream Parlor, then later at Lax Auto Supply where she, as a front counter clerk, was responsible for locating parts for customers. After Pearl raised the amount she was charging for room and board, Myrt felt she was being forced to choose the workplace over school, which she eventually did, ending her formal education at the tenth grade. It was a decision she would long regret. Later, Myrt moved out of her mother's home and rented a room. On the hunt for better employment opportunities, she took a position as a bookkeeper at Leopold & Price, a men's clothing store. She was living on her own and working as a bookkeeper when she and a few girlfriends crowded into a booth at The Quality Sandwich Shop and she first set eyes on her future husband.

Vince and Myrt

Before they'd even spoken to each other, Myrt was strongly attracted to Vince. He had left her with a surprisingly powerful first impression and she could not quite forget him. Later, her friends returned to The Quality Sandwich Shop (without Myrt for she was out on a date) and they met up with the Baylor boys. Afterward, buzzing with news, the girls told Myrt about the encounter. Myrt wanted to know about the one with the squinty eyes. Yes, the girls reported, he was there and no, he didn't seem to be attached to anyone. Myrt was present on the next visit to the diner and there was Vince. While sitting in the booth with her girlfriends, Myrt got something in her eye. Could you be a little less obvious? the other girls laughed. Myrt protested that she actually *did* have something in her eye, and it hurt too. That was when second year medical student Vince Somers came over to see if he might be of assistance.

Vince and Myrt at the place of their first meeting with pal Charlie Meadows and his date. (*Hume family collection*)

In spite of Vince's heavy school workload, he and Myrt found many opportunities to spend time together. They went to parties at the fraternity house and attended those thrown by the dental school students, which were consistently the best parties. They took trips to Galveston and visited the beach. They did a lot of dancing too. Sometimes the dance floor would empty so Vince and Myrt could perform the jitterbug alone before an admiring group of onlookers. Almost immediately Myrt was smitten. Vince was intelligent, fun, and cute. He was adventuresome too, speaking of his dreams of becoming a frontier doctor in Alaska. He seemed to be the perfect man with which to begin a future. His occupational pursuit pointed to financial security as well. It would be a privilege and honor to be married to a man as fine as Vince. But there was one big drawback. Vince was involved with another woman, since before he had met Myrt, and he told her as much. Later, when Vince broached the subject of marriage with Myrt, she refused to entertain any serious thought of it as long as he was involved with someone else.

He broke up with his other girlfriend, but stayed in contact through telephone conversations. Sometimes he shared his misgivings regarding the engagement to Myrt. He wondered if he was really ready for marriage. Sure Myrt was kind, fun, and a beautiful woman and he thought it was fine that she had no career aspirations, wanting instead to be a full-time wife and mother. And her sense of loyalty was beyond reproach—an important character element to Vince. The only thing "wrong" with her was she was the same height as him, taller with heels. But what did that really matter? Still, he wondered if he and Myrt were moving the relationship ahead too fast. At last Vince asked his ex-girlfriend for her thoughts. She pointed out that it was easier to end an engagement than a marriage, and if he wasn't sure that he could see the marriage through, then he should break the engagement. It was really as simple as that, she said. Vince agreed; it was that simple. He would marry Myrt.

Without question, Vince's choice in a spouse was instrumental in furthering his occupational pursuits. That's not to say that he did not marry for love, but additionally, cognitively or not, he, like other medical students or practicing physicians, was looking for a person who would complement the subject of his lifelong investment: his profession. The ideal wife was one who needn't be worried about, would not be a distraction from the work, and who would not easily succumb to jealousy. She needed to be a partner who understood she would be sharing her spouse with a community—a community which believed that he belonged to it as much as to her. She would need to accept that some female patients would feel attracted to his status and powers of healing. She had to be forgiving of missed dates and interruptions into those special events he could attend. The doctor's wife had to be self-sufficient, capable of running and maintaining a household on her own, and competent to raise children, also often on her own. She would have to try to make up for his absences and offer explanations for missed family and school events. Her life and their children's would have to be centered around the one who wasn't there. Myrt, he knew, would be up to the task.

Several bits of business were conducted prior to the wedding. First, Vince entered into the process of having his surname changed back to Hume. This was at the request of his father, John Hume, who had been providing regular financial contributions to Vince's education. It seemed only right to John that if he was helping his son through a costly private medical school, then that son should at least bear his name. The papers went before the court, this time changing Vince's name to include both surnames: Vincent Harrington Somers Hume. The couple also had to find a way to raise funds to pay for the wedding. Increasing their income seemed impossible as Myrt was already working full-time, and Vince was going to school full-time plus working odd jobs whenever possible. But Vince had a solution up his sleeve, quite literally. He possessed a rare blood type which was much in demand and therefore valuable. So Vince sold his blood as often as allowed, a pint every six weeks, to raise money for the wedding.

After Catechism classes, Myrt joined the Catholic faith, which allowed her and Vince to marry in the church. The ceremony occurred on February 20, 1948 at St. Mary's Catholic Church in Houston. It was a small, modest wedding with only a few friends and family members in attendance. Older brother Henry Bush gave Myrt away. On the way down the aisle, faced with the enormity of the event, the bride got a momentary case of cold feet, and pulled away slightly from her brother. She whispered that maybe she didn't want to go through with the marriage after all, that maybe she should just walk away. Henry, knowing his sister's heart, wisely pulled her back to his side and whispered, "Oh, no you don't."

Following an abbreviated honeymoon, more on the order of a long weekend, the newlyweds settled into an upstairs two-room garage apartment. The floor plan was simple, an open room that contained a bed, a small kitchen and living area, and a separate bathroom. It was sparse but sufficient for a medical school student and his bride.

Myrt's introduction to her in-laws was very positive. She liked them all, but the man whom she would grow to love like a father was John Hume. With the passing of her own father still fresh in her memory, the kindness, generosity, and friendship that John extended to Myrt touched her deeply.

The Upperclassman

The building program at Baylor neared completion. The project had bogged down several times due to cost overruns and other factors before Mr. Hugh Roy Cullen, a Houston oil ty-

coon, got involved. Cullen gave Baylor an unbelievably generous financial donation that covered the entire program's costs.

The summer between Vince's sophomore and junior years
did not include a job hunt. He and his Baylor classmates were
employed in moving the contents of the school from the Sears
building to the new facility. The new school was a structure to
behold. Rising above M.D. Anderson Boulevard, the massive
reinforced concrete, granite, and limestone Roy and Lillie Cullen Building was the new home of Baylor University College
of Medicine. The building was nothing short of a showplace
to even the most casual observer of architecture, but especially for those students who had attended Baylor in the modest
Sears and Roebuck quarters. The Cullen Building was more
than 130,000 square feet of air-conditioned white, polish, and
shine. As they said of it then, "This is uptown." The new school
had more than an impressive exterior. The students benefited
from upgrades to equipment and even had professionally dis-
sected cadavers in the labs. The grand building had more of everything. Baylor's distinguished level of instruction remained,
but the institution's profile now matched its quality. For the
students, faculty, administration, community of Houston, and
even the state of Texas, Baylor school pride ran high.

The Roy and Lillie Cullen Building, Baylor University College of Medicine. (*A
History of Baylor University College of Medicine 1900-1953*)

The focus of Vince's freshman and sophomore years had
been courses in basic medical science. For his junior and senior
years, the courses were in clinical studies, with a greater emphasis on physical diagnosis and surgery. On a typical school
day, Vince's morning classes consisted of four lectures. In the
afternoon, he worked at Veterans Hospital, a Baylor affiliate.
Under watchful supervision, his work at Veterans Hospital gave

Vince valuable hands-on training in patient care and other medical skills.

On the Job Training

His training began with patients who humbly came seeking help. They may have been anxious, in pain, or even fearing death. It was Vince's duty to see patients through their period of illness. As a doctor he was to cure when possible, alleviate symptoms when it was not possible to cure, and finally, to console when he could do no more. He would find it a highly intimate relationship.

In the maintenance and care of a patient's body, Vince would diagnose illness, deliver babies, perform surgery, repair fractures and dislocations, and write prescriptions. He would give hypodermic injections, handle internal organs, and deal with blood and other bodily fluids. As a doctor he would provide patients and family members with information that might be good or bad. He would manage a healthcare team that might include, among others, nurses, technicians, and pharmacists. His management duties extended to the administration of office staff, insurance issues, and governmental regulations. Vince would have to learn to perform all these functions in an efficient manner, for there was no shortage of need.

An Inexact Science

Through lecture and study, Vince had learned the basis of what would become perhaps his greatest asset in the field of medicine: his ability to diagnose illness. At Veterans Hospital, for the first time, he put this knowledge into practice.

Diagnosis, from Greek origins, meaning to discern and distinguish, could be a tremendously complicated process. It was only through study, practice, observation, and even intuition that consistently correct diagnoses were attained. At the time Vince entered the profession in the late 1940s, the lack of modern diagnostic tests and equipment necessitated a greater reliance on the traditional art of diagnosis. Vince learned to ply his art in small examination rooms, employing his greatest tool in diagnosis—listening. Patients generally told him, through symptom descriptions, the nature of their problem. He interviewed patients in an attempt to coax further information; information that in some cases they felt was too embarrassing, or that they were too fearful to report. Vince had to establish confidence and build a rapport with each patient to extract important information. He would give his patient a physical exam which might include palpation (examination by touch) and auscultation (listening, by stethoscope, to the functioning of internal organs). The physical examination also included body temperature and blood pressure measurements. The patient may have undergone physical tests which Vince interpreted. If warranted, blood or other fluids might have been obtained for further testing. He may have ordered x-rays. In making a diagnosis, again under careful supervision, Vince would review the results of a physical examination and evaluate laboratory data. He also considered the patient's medical history and even that of family members for possible diseases linked to heredity. To complicate matters, a patient might be suffering from two or even more diseases simultaneously, with one condition's symptoms masking or modifying the others. In a comprehensive diagnostic effort, Vince often made "differential diagnoses," listing several conclusions ranked by highest probability. Differential diagnoses may have prompted further examinations or testing. From all of this, Vince had to decide on a course of patient care. The chosen course of action may have even been no action at all, for in many cases the body would heal itself over time. Sometimes Vince would suggest a change in diet or personal habits. He might prescribe medication. Another option was surgery.

On Surgery, Judgment, and Ego

Vince learned that a surgeon's real abilities and skills lie chiefly in his judgment *prior* to surgery. Of primary concern was arriving at an accurate diagnosis so that a useful surgery could be performed. He learned that the surgeon also had to weigh probabilities of success verses failure in the best interest of the patient. Any surgery could hardly be considered successful if the patient's heart was not of sufficient strength to withstand the operation or recovery period. The surgeon was not only to judge if he should operate, but when as well, for some patients needed time to gain strength before undergoing a procedure. In such a situation, a surgeon would be required to perform the surgery during that window of opportunity when the patient's strength was at its attainable peak and while the cause or need for the surgery was most manageable. Another part of judgment, Vince learned, was balancing one's ego.

Surgeons needed confidence to perform at the full extent of their capabilities. They had to know they were up to the mighty task before them and that they were the best doctor for the job, for the operating room was no place for the scared or meek. Armed with sufficient ego, the skilled surgeon endeavored to keep it in check. They were fully aware of the invasiveness of surgery and its inherent risks. They were conscious that in many instances surgery was only an option—that patients might well enjoy a full recovery on their own. For those reasons they understood that in some cases the only benefit from surgery was in misplaced credit for healing.

The Nurses

The field of nursing, in terms of function and occupational culture, was another area of medicine which Vince was exposed to during his training at Veterans Hospital.

Nursing duties were many and varied, and the level of responsibility assumed was often as much as an individual was willing to accept. A hospital nurse's general duties included, foremost, the continuous care of several patients. This included administering prescribed medications and "charting" or recording medications given. The importance of this aspect of a nurse's work could not be overstressed, for accurate charting was absolutely imperative in patient care. Nurses were responsible for monitoring and recording the patient's ongoing health status when a physician was not present. They changed dressings and assisted the patient with hygiene. They served meals. They worked in the hospital labs and performed a multitude of obstetric duties. They seemed to always be cleaning something in an effort to stave off infection. In a time before disposable healthcare products, they were tasked with the sterilization of equipment. Everything from bedpans and catheters to needles and syringes were sterilized by boiling, steam, or soaking in disinfectant. This was not a simple or haphazard process, as each item had an approved method and procedure for sterilization. They sharpened hypodermic needles. They made ready operating rooms, assembled all necessary instruments, and assisted in surgery.

Expectations were not limited to the successful completion of their assigned duties. They had an image to uphold as well, based largely on personal appearance. It started with the cap, a form of nursing I.D. These white caps were worn at all times and were affixed to the hair with white bobby pins. Nursing uniforms were to be sharply starched and snow white. Stockings or hose were also white. The shoes, white, were either the flat "clinical" type or those outfitted with oversized heels. The shoes required the most time in maintenance for they had to be kept polished to the point of shining. A nurse's hair was to be worn off the collar and her face was to be free of makeup. The fingernails were not to extend beyond the fingertips and the nails were to be without nail polish. This image of an immaculately attired healthcare professional was not only important to the nursing profession in general, but also directly reflected upon the facility where they were employed. The nursing staff in many ways was the face of the institution.

Another important aspect of nursing was the relationship between the nurse and the patient. Nurses were often the first point of contact for those seeking medical treatment. As such, a nurse, from the very outset, was expected to display confidence in herself and the facility, in an attempt to put the patient at ease. This ability to impart confidence and calm was most useful in the emergency room where a nurse was expected to remain composed in the face of sometimes unbelievable human trauma. In less extreme situations, the nurse served as a kind of unofficial liaison between the patient and the doctor. Nurses seemed to be in less of a rush and more accessible than a doctor. After all, a doctor would come to the hospital and make rounds only to leave again for private practice while nursing care was continuous with a seemingly greater investment in the patient and their employer, the hospital.

Though in pursuit of a common goal, conflict frequently arose in the professional relationship between physician and nurse. Nurses were easily subjected to educational or social status intimidation from a doctor. Feelings of intimidation may have been self-imposed, for nurses were keenly aware of a doctor's superior education and position in the community, but sometimes they stemmed from a doctor's behavior. A doctor, especially a surgeon, generally had a well-developed ego.

Ego, coupled with a lifestyle that was harried and short on rest, were all the ingredients necessary for the dispensing of caustic remarks. Sometimes nurses jokingly remarked that a physician had taken "a course in God" while in medical school. But for all the personal and professional conflicts that did exist in this decidedly stressful profession, it is surprising that there wasn't even more. Several factors, however, contributed to what may be called a "professional détente." Doctors valued nurses highly, especially those they considered to be good ones. The good ones were typified as intelligent, efficient, reliable, and prepared. The good ones also looked after the doctor's best interests. They smoothed out uncomfortable matters with patients and other nurses on the doctor's behalf. They provided support through encouragement, and by performing small tasks for the physician. Sometimes they made excuses for them too. This was an aspect of their training. Nurses were taught deference in their professional relationships with doctors. If sitting, nurses had been taught to stand when a doctor entered a patient's room. If a nurse was sitting at the nurse's station and a doctor arrived, the nurse had been taught to rise and offer the doctor her chair. Nurses, as they had been instructed, always referred to and addressed the physician by title and surname. The fact that deference was *taught* rather than allowed to foster naturally would seem to imply that there was a sort of falseness to it all. Usually this was not the case. Nurses respected doctors and wished them well, even if at times they were frustrated by their behavior. The relationships were something akin to family.

Day After Day

Vince and Myrt still didn't have much money, even though Myrt was working full-time and John Hume had raised Vince's stipend to $110 a month after the wedding. They were getting by, but there wasn't much room for error in the budget. This explains their not upgrading from "Dysmenorrhea." Dysmenorrhea, a Greek medical term meaning painful menstruation, was the frat boys' nickname for the Hume's great, black 1937 Packard. Having long since seen its better days, the car looked bad and ran worse. It usually required a push start and when the engine got too warm it ceased to run at all. Vince had originally paid $122 for it, and one more dollar toward the maintenance of the beast would have been good money after bad, so they just drove it whenever it would run.

The couple settled into a routine. Myrt got up in the morning and headed down to a nearby bus stop to catch the bus that would take her to Leopold & Price, where she had risen to the position of head bookkeeper. Vince would get Dysmenorrhea started and swing through his route to school, picking up classmates along the way. After work and school each would return home and Vince would study late into the night. If the next day's schedule included a test, he sometimes studied all night, knocking off at around 5 A.M. to sleep for one or two hours before getting up and heading to school to take his exam. This method seemed to work well for him, as he always scored high on his tests. Myrt was amazed by her husband's ability to take in information and retain it. She was amazed at his self-discipline and focus in attaining his goals. She was amazed too when he broke the news to her that he may have fathered a child years previously.

During one of the many periods when he wasn't staying with his family, living instead with a married couple, Vince was asked by the husband if he might be willing to sleep with his wife. Vince agreed and later the woman gave birth to a child. There existed the possibility that the child belonged to Vince. After telling Myrt the story, Vince suggested that perhaps they could find the child, ascertain parentage, and if it indeed was his, then raise the child. Myrt said no. After all, they were still just newlyweds, and she didn't feel prepared for such a sudden and radical change. From time to time, other issues from Vince's strange past, some great and some small, surfaced and required healing and understanding. Those issues were handled between Vince and Myrt. Outsiders who witnessed a manifestation of some past event would be told nothing of the private matter, or would be told a story more in fitting with the social graces—or at least something that seemed "normal." The most obvious example that played out during this period in their lives was Vince's name change back to Hume. Vince's Baylor buddies were told that he had been given the name Somers after his parents' messy divorce, with no mention of the family's years on the lam eluding State, Federal, and International law enforcement officials. Those kinds of stories required too much explanation.

The remainder of Vince's junior year and his senior year passed quickly. Looking back at his years at the school, he could not have helped noticing some ironic changes. Many of his former Hot Wells High School classmates wouldn't have dreamt that their bright, but not particularly scholastically-motivated, friend Vinnie would have begun, much less finished, medical school. Similarly, they wouldn't have thought that their fun-loving old friend would have chosen such a serious profession. The girls he dated wouldn't have believed he could get serious enough about any girl to marry. But here he was, a married man on the cusp of becoming a medical doctor.

Graduation Day

June 13, 1949 was the big day and Vince's family was in town. Spirits were high for the gala event. The women were all dressed up. Vince's mother, the height-conscious Gracie, ventured a question regarding Myrt's choice in footwear or, more specifically, her choice in heel thickness. Myrt, who was the same height as Vince when they were first married, had continued to grow, rising an inch above her husband (to his slight chagrin) and she was much taller than the diminutive Gracie. A kind of "height accord" was reached when it was agreed that Gracie would stand next to Doreen instead of Myrt at the ceremony.

The Grad. Vince Hume 1949.
(Hume family collection)

The Baylor University College of Medicine commencement exercises were held in the auditorium of the school. Vince and sixty-one of his fellow graduates entered the great hall to the sound of *Pomp and Circumstance* and stood for the invocation by Reverend Shirkey of St. Paul's Methodist Church. The graduates, and their family and friends, were seated for the address presented by William Vermillion Houston, President of Rice University. Next came the conferring of degrees and presentation of diplomas. This was followed by the benediction, offered by Reverend Knowles of the First Christian Church. And it was all over. Their greatest goal had been accomplished. They had earned the right, through arduous study and experience, to serve their fellow man. At graduation they were given one last piece of vital information before setting forth in their profession. It was a code of ethics—The Hippocratic Oath.

Devised by the Greek physician Hippocrates, sometimes referred to as "The Father of Medicine," the oath reads, in part:

I will apply dietetic measures for the benefit of the sick according to my ability and judgment; I will keep them from harm and injustice.

I will neither give a deadly drug to anybody who asked for it, nor will I make a suggestion to this effect. In purity and holiness I will guard my life and art.

Whatever houses I may visit, I will come for the benefit of the sick, remaining free of all intentional injustice, of all mischief and in particular of sexual relations with both female and male persons.

What I may see or hear in the course of the treatment or even outside the treatment in regard to the life of men, which on no account one must spread abroad, I will keep to myself, holding such shameful to be spoken about.

If I fulfill this oath and do not violate it, may it be granted to me to enjoy life and art, being honored with fame among men for all time to come; if I transgress it and swear falsely, may the opposite of all this be my lot.

5

The Medical Corps

Tripler

Weighing his options for an internship in 1949, Dr. Hume chose the U.S. Army. Several factors were involved in this decision. One was financial. The Army needed doctors and was paying thirty dollars a month plus housing. The salary was at least equal to that offered in civilian hospitals, but the housing benefits in addition to the Post Exchange (PX) privileges of the Army made it the better offer. Dr. Hume had enlisted in the Reserve Officer Training Corps (ROTC) while attending Baylor and received his commission as a First Lieutenant on graduation day. After beginning active duty, he was to be first stationed at Tripler General Hospital on the island of Oahu, Hawaii.

Dr. Hume took the state medical board examination in Austin, a grueling three-day written test, then departed for Hawaii almost immediately, leaving Myrt to wrap up the loose ends of the move and join him in a couple of weeks. One of those loose ends concerned the sale of Dysmenorrhea, their hulking Packard. Myrt was of the opinion that they would either have no luck in selling the car or would receive virtually nothing for it. They originally bought the car, well used, for $122, but now it was worth less. Much less. Still in terrible running condition but now with more body damage and broken windows to add to its cosmetic woes, moving the vehicle, literally or figuratively, seemed hopeless. Dr. Hume had the solution: have Grover sell it. True to form, Grover Bates, the ultimate salesman, sold Dysmenorrhea for a handsome profit. With the doctor gone, Myrt finished preparations for the move and boarded a train for California. From there she embarked on the final leg of her journey to Hawaii via a five-day excursion aboard ship. This was the first time she had been outside of Texas.

Seated on Moanalua Ridge, the coral pink hued Tripler General Hospital was an eye-catching sight on the island's south shore. It was new facility completed less than a year before the Humes arrived. In fact, Dr. Hume was among the first group of twenty graduates, fourteen Army and six Navy, to serve in the hospital's intern training program. Work in the program was continual, with very few off-duty hours, but the experience was wonderful and the young Dr. Hume reveled in the challenge. Described by his superior officers as alert, interested, and anxious to learn all phases of medicine, he was the model intern. When a voluntary test in internal medicine was offered to all residents and interns at Tripler, Dr. Hume was the only intern to sit for the examination. He made one of the highest scores on the test. His superiors and colleagues also quickly noticed he was coolheaded and confident in emergency situations. He was also known for his friendly and cheerful demeanor. His hard work continued to pay off; just prior to Christmas he received the test results he had been waiting for—the Texas State Board of Medical Examiners officially licensed him to practice medicine.

Dr. Hume and Myrt's accommodations were in the recently vacated single story hospital barracks of Fort Shafter. The barracks were generally without partitions, which offered plenty of room. Too much room. The quarters, not intended as single family dwellings, were so impossibly large that the Humes hung blankets to separate their living area from the remaining expanse of empty space. Their daily routine found the doctor at Tripler and Myrt employed at the PX. Their time together was limited by his schedule, but they still found time to play bridge with neighbors. The doctor was able to get away to play golf on occasion, and Myrt took lessons in the sport until she was no longer comfortable swinging a golf club—for Myrt was with child.

The doctor was delighted to learn Myrt was pregnant. They were both excited to start a family. Following an easy pregnancy, Myrt gave birth to their first child, a daughter they named April, in 1950 in Honolulu.

The young family's tenure was growing short in Hawaii. The doctor had nearly completed his one year of rotating internship. He had already received his next assignment to serve at Madigan

Army Hospital in Tacoma, Washington. He left Tripler with the same high marks on his Officer Efficiency Report that had become the hallmark of his stay at Tripler, and he left with a promotion.

Captain Vincent Hume, M.C.

The flight, Myrtle's first, back to the States was a terrifying experience. Flying in a small, noisy, propeller-driven military transport, and seated in uncomfortable canvas sling chairs, the Humes were deep into the flight over the seemingly endless open water when the plane began to encounter mechanical difficulties. Eventually, the flight crew determined that the safest course of action was to return to Hawaii, which they did, after thirteen hours of airtime in the failed attempt to reach the mainland. After a brief respite, the Humes took to the air once more, with apprehension, and completed their marathon journey.

Located on Washington's scenic Puget Sound, Fort Lewis, named after Meriwether Lewis of the Lewis & Clark expedition, is home to Madigan Army Hospital. This was Dr. Hume's place of work for the duration of his residency program. He began his rotating residency with duties that included responsibilities for ward personnel, and carrying out all preoperative and postoperative orders on patients. He gave physical examinations and took medical histories. He assisted in surgery and was allowed to perform some procedures under supervision. The hours were long, but the young doctor was more than up to the task. Medical associates found him well-mannered, unassuming, and dependable. Superiors praised his initiative and constant striving to improve professionally. Later he moved into Obstetric and Gynecology services where he received similar high marks from colleagues and rating officers. He found his work particularly fascinating while serving in the hospital's Psychiatric Ward. Here his superiors commended his efforts to avail himself of all educational opportunities, even in areas where he didn't plan to specialize. It was quite clear Dr. Hume loved to learn and loved being a doctor.

Dr. Hume loved his wife and family too. Upon arrival in Tacoma, he and Myrt first lived in a civilian apartment but soon moved onto Fort Lewis into newly constructed physicians' housing. From money they saved in Hawaii, they purchased a brand new Chevrolet and the doctor taught Myrt how to drive. The lesson took place on a Sunday and lasted just two and a half hours. Apparently that was enough. The next day Myrt wheeled out onto Highway 90 and took the doctor to work. Dropping him at Madigan, she cruised over to the commissary, the PX, and the post office before returning home in the great American freedom machine. For fun, Myrt and the doctor attended parties at the officers' club and shared time at home, where Dr. Hume was an attentive father. But his time at home was generally brief. Despite his love for his family, and even with another child on the way, domestic life could not compete with the intellectually stimulating and sometimes adrenalin-fueled work at the hospital. Nothing could. When he did have time off, he wanted to completely unwind without encumbrances, often through golf, at which he now excelled. Sometimes he had a few drinks.

Drinking seemed a good fit with the military lifestyle: young men, full of testosterone, sought quick camaraderie through the use of the great social elixir. Due to the inherent risks of being a soldier, the socially accepted rules of moderate drinking did not seem to apply—not when the very individual seeking a drink might soon be placed in harm's way in service to his country. If servicemen, both enlisted men and officers, felt that overindulgence was a rite of passage, especially in time of war, then military doctors were given to thinking, even in peacetime, it was their *right*. There was no one to tell them differently. Doctors, especially surgeons, were of such tremendous value to the military that much bad behavior was overlooked. In many instances they received a pass on disciplinary actions.

In late August of 1951, another daughter, Dawn, was born to the great joy of her parents. Shortly after this new arrival, the doctor made a shocking revelation. He told Myrt that he had been repeatedly unfaithful. He shared the disturbing news with her as if he was merely passing on a bit of routine information. Myrt was more confused by the manner of the declaration than its content. The doctor's great charisma had, for some time, contained a strong element of promiscuity, a certain air of availability, but what was she to make of his disclosure? Was he trying to motivate her into leaving him? Was he trying to clear his conscience? Was he testing her? His intentions remained unclear, and Myrt made plans to leave him. Then she discovered she was pregnant again, less than three months after giving birth to Dawn. Their third child and first son, Frank, was born on August 18, 1952 in Tacoma. Three months after Frank's birth, Myrt was pregnant again, earning her the nickname of "Fertile Myrtle." She gave up thoughts of leaving her husband.

The doctor's career continued its smooth ascent. He served on the medical board at Madigan. He readily took on responsibility and demonstrated his substantial abilities by working quickly and effectively. He seemed to never tire. He established an outstanding rapport with his patients and remained popular with his colleagues. His progress in the residency program was termed excellent.

Back to Texas

With his residency complete, Dr. Hume was given orders to report to Brooke Army Medical Center at Fort Sam Houston. He was to attend the Center's Medical Field Service School in preparation for service overseas.

The move brought him and Myrt back to familiar surroundings. The doctor was able to renew his relationship with sister Doreen, and Myrt with her family as well. Myrt's mother, Pearl, stayed with the Humes for a time soon after their arrival to provide assistance in the latter phase of Myrt's pregnancy. Pearl was dismayed with the doctor's absence from home and his drinking, and she told him as much. The relationship between Pearl and the doctor quickly soured. The Hume's fourth child,

The growing Hume family. Clockwise from Myrt: Dawn, Frank, Cindy, and April. (*Hume family collection*)

Cindy, was born on August 30, 1953 in San Antonio. She was the image of her father, much to the doctor's delight. With four children under the age of three-and-a-half, Myrt was busy, to say the least. Their living quarters didn't help. The brand new building had no landscaping; there was no lawn, only dirt. By Myrt's count, the record for baths given to her children in one day was sixteen. She did almost all the work alone, the doctor being off in his professional pursuits. Even when he wasn't working, he wasn't at home. He played golf, fished for bass, and hunted quail. His leisure pursuits were his own. In the context of the times, this was not unusual. This was an era in which there was an unfair but clear demarcation of duties between husband and wife.

His medical field service training in Texas lasted seven months. Upon completion, his academic ranking placed him in the top third of the class. Dr. Hume, along with Myrt and the four kids, were bound for Germany.

Europe

The doctor, now a Major, arrived first in the town of Garmisch, Germany. Located in southern Germany in the Upper Bavarian Loisachtal Valley, it was a place of astounding alpine beauty. In addition to many natural wonders, the area boasted nearby castle ruins, wonderful old churches, and the more modern architecture of the Olympic Ice Stadium constructed for the 1936 Olympic Games. Myrt and the children arrived a month after Dr. Hume. The accommodations were splendid. They lived in a large home served by a staff of three—a gardener, a maintenance man, and Agata, the full-time maid. The trusted Agata often stayed with the children, allowing the couple, particularly Myrt, greater freedom in travel and other activities. Myrt especially enjoyed skiing, which the doctor tried too, and as a sign of his continued agility, he picked up the sport after only a few outings. The doctor and Myrt enjoyed entertaining friends and acquaintances in their Garmisch home. They experienced many travel opportunities that being stationed in Europe afforded. They toured France, Holland, Italy, and Austria by automobile.

Dr. Hume's work at the Garmisch Sub Area Dispensary was lauded by his direct superior officer who noted in him a professional competence of a caliber rarely found in a medical officer his age. He was also commended for his devotion to his patients and their fondness for him. Another officer, up the chain of command, who had less frequent contact with Dr. Hume, was not so enamored. He found Dr. Hume to have a sometimes impetuous manner in his personal relationships. He also thought that he lacked some of the polish and poise expected in a doctor. He said Dr. Hume was the type best suited for field hospital work during combat, where his strength of force-

On the Italian Riviera. (*Hume family collection*)

ful leadership in emergency situations could be best utilized. This was the doctor's harshest criticism, really his first, to date. The remarks concerning poise and polish may have stemmed from incidents like the missed General's reception. A Christmas reception was given for eight visiting Generals. Dr. Hume was to be in attendance, as were several other doctors. Prior to the evening party Dr. Hume, along with another doctor and a dentist, went out for haircuts and never returned for the reception, opting instead to go out drinking. Nothing was said at the time to Dr. Hume or the others—these were, after all, doctors. But it was the kind of thing that might be remembered.

Another transfer was ordered, this time sending the Humes to Ulm, Germany, on the banks of the Danube River. The family's Ulm housing, a small apartment, was not nearly as comfortable as they'd enjoyed in Garmisch, but at least they were able to bring the much-loved Agata along. The doctor was stationed in Ulm and served as a commanding officer in the 22nd Medical Detachment. Additionally, he functioned as a Post surgeon. In his tenure at Ulm, lasting eight months, he was given mixed marks for his performance. Those rating him (infantry officers, not those from the medical corps) found him excellent in the administration of his dispensary and detachment, but less skilled when dealing with his professional associates. They also criticized his military bearing and appearance—criticisms of a surprisingly personal nature. In a later evaluation, improvements in those areas were reported and in general more positive marks were given, but his promotion potential was downgraded by both reviewing officers. The doctor requested a transfer from Ulm to a field hospital, which would reduce his administrative duties and allow him to focus more on his profession.

The change of scenery did wonders for him. Stationed in Augsburg, Germany and serving as Chief of General Surgery, he was described as displaying unusual initiative and diligence. He was said to have a very pleasing personality and was tactful in interactions with patients and subordinates. His next Officer Efficiency Report confirmed as much and elaborated that he was energetic, conscientious, and indefatigable. Further, the evaluation stated that few other officers could attain his level of performance. Another review section stated he was one of the few highly outstanding officers the rater knew. Under the Estimated Desirability in Various Capacities section, he scored the maximum, five out of five in all nine reporting categories. As a final tip of the hat to Dr. Hume, the evaluation praised his considerable administrative abilities. Down, but not out, while in Ulm, he had responded in a positive and professional manner to great result in Augsburg.

While stationed in Augsburg, the doctor and his wife traveled to Cortina d'Ampezzo, Italy to take in the 1956 Olympic Winter Games, while Agata watched the kids. It was a historic Olympics due to the first-ever appearance by a team from the USSR.

The Humes attended bobsledding, slalom skiing, and skating events. To see one of the events, they had to climb a long, steep slope to the viewing area. The doctor, who had a plantar wart on his foot, was in some discomfort making the climb. As a bus passed the crowd ascending the slope, the doctor seized the opportunity. Reaching out in a flash of the old Vinnie, he grabbed a ladder attached to the rear of the bus and hoisted himself on board as the vehicle made its way to the top. Myrt finally made it to the viewing area, only to find that she had arrived too late and had missed the event. The doctor was able to tell her all about it; he hadn't missed a thing.

One day, shortly after the Italy trip, three-and-a-half year old Frank told his mother of a "funny sound" in his head, a sound like an airplane. When told of this, Dr. Hume listened with a stethoscope and indeed detected a hum in Frank's head. Frank was taken to Munich to see a host of experts including pediatricians and neurosurgeons. All came to the conclusion that Frank had an aneurysm. The doctor and Myrt, acting on the specialists' advice and under tremendous stress, made immediate plans to take Frank back to the States to Walter Reed Hospital.

The trip was something of a logistic military nightmare. First, they packed their belongings and secured shipping. The Army had anticipated two separate flights: the doctor traveling with the three little girls, and Myrt making the trip with Frank. The Humes thought it made better sense for the doctor to travel with Frank in case the boy needed medical attention, with Myrt journeying with the girls. After some confusion by the Army as to how the travel arrangements could be altered, the trip was underway. The first leg of the trip took them to New Jersey. Myrt and the girls arrived first and met each new arriving flight in anticipation of meeting Frank and the doctor. Finally the family learned that the Army had arranged transportation on to Washington, D.C. and Walter Reed Hospital for the doctor and Frank, but the rest of the family was on its own. Myrt looked up a family friend in New Jersey and sold him the family car, which was en route from Germany. With those proceeds, she purchased a Chevrolet and set out with the girls for Washington, D.C. Along the way, she became impossibly lost, adding many more hours to the trip, all the while wondering how her son was faring. At last she was reunited with the doctor and Frank, and learned that the medical tests had determined nothing was wrong with Frank. The doctors in Germany had been mistaken as to the seriousness; the hum they had heard in Frank was common and not life threatening. With the passing of Frank's health scare, the family members prepared to resume their lives. The Army issued Dr. Hume orders to report to El Paso, Texas.

Back in the USA

Arriving in El Paso, the Humes were surprised to learn that Army officials knew nothing of Dr. Hume's transfer. Inquiries were made, but officials could find nothing indicating the Humes should be there. Maybe, they suggested, the doctor should report to Fort Sam Houston. Sensing a military runaround, Myrt and the kids stayed in Houston until the matter of where the doctor was to be stationed was sorted out. The doctor's disenchantment with the military was rapidly increasing. After much uncertainty, his orders came through; he was assigned to Brooke Army Hospital at Fort Sam Houston. By now his heart was no longer in it. He continued to provide excellent patient care as a medical officer working in outpatient services, but now he had something else in mind—the fulfillment of his long-held dream of living in Alaska.

In late July of 1956 Dr. Hume resigned from the Army. The weeks ahead were filled with plans and preparations for the trip north as well as saying goodbye to friends and family. Grover and Gracie visited the Humes during this period. While visiting, Grover made a point of telling the doctor that he noticed in him a proclivity for overindulgence with alcohol. When the doctor protested, Grover upped the ante and told him outright, "You've got that John Barleycorn on your back."

6

John Barleycorn

Alcoholic Memoirs

When Grover Bates invoked the name John Barleycorn to warn Dr. Hume, his stepson, of the dangers of alcohol abuse, he was citing a phrase that had come to be known as the embodiment of intoxicating liquor. The phrase originates from a Robert Burns ballad, later adapted into an English drinking song. It was also the title of Jack London's semiautobiographical novel, *John Barleycorn: Alcoholic Memoirs*. The book praises alcohol as a kind of social tonic that promotes lively fellowship. Alcohol receives romantic treatment, espousing the glamour of experiencing life "glass in hand." But it all dissolves into a study of the insidious nature of alcohol's grip on the individual and the painful realities of London's own self-acknowledged alcoholism. The book provides firsthand insight into the developmental stages of alcoholism and addictive behaviors. For these reasons, the book earned accolades for promoting an understanding of its subject matter, but it did little to influence the ongoing, often heated debate over whether alcoholism was a disease.

The Declaration

The World Health Organization got the ball rolling by recognizing that alcoholism was a significant medical problem in 1951. Five years later, the American Medical Association made a monumental declaration. In a resolution, the AMA granted alcoholism official status as a treatable disease. This groundbreaking resolution carried substantial ramifications. With the change in medical thought on the subject came the legitimization of alcohol programs, treatment plans, and research.

What Makes it a Disease?

In order for the AMA to declare alcoholism a disease, the malady had to meet the Association's criteria for disease designation. The AMA ruled that alcoholism could be described through symptoms: a change in the subject's personality; a change in the pattern of consumption; a preoccupation with alcohol; physical, psychological, or social problems brought on by alcohol use; a change in alcohol tolerance levels; and a loss of control. The ruling also stated that the disease of alcoholism was chronic, that its course was predictable and progressive, that it was a primary illness, and that it was treatable.

The Cause

Although the results of alcoholism are apparent, the cause is more elusive. In the absence of hard data supporting a specific cause of alcoholism, theory-based grounds for the disease were employed. One approach suggested the disease was passed down through heredity. Another view with a genetic-based approach proposed that some individuals metabolized alcohol in a way that increased their likelihood of becoming alcoholics. Factors relating to issues of family and personal environment were advanced. More consideration was given to behavioral-based thought as researchers began to realize that biological and behavioral approaches could interconnect in defining a cause for alcoholism. Among behavior-based theories were ideas that some may become victims of the disease by using alcohol to control feelings of stress or anxiety. Another theory held that excessive consumption of alcohol actually caused the brain to function differently. Those subscribing to this theory believed the brain's motivational paths were subverted into a priority system that ranked alcohol first. While new theories were being advanced, researchers were also compiling empirical evidence about the developmental stages of alcoholism.

You **Can** Get There From Here

The developmental stages of alcoholism are common to almost all its sufferers. With all the information available both in print and through personal experience, one might think that an individual would be able to self-diagnose and take action to stop any advancement. But the development of alcoholism is almost seamless as it moves from stage to stage. The warning signs are obvious, to be sure, but they seem to be visible to the abuser only in retrospect. For active alcoholics, the honeymoon period with alcohol is one of their most cherished memories. The substance has acted as a social lubricant, helping to draw out, they believe, their most attractive self—engaging and funny for some, brave and outspoken for others. In the beginning, alcohol may have served as the tonic needed to get over life's rough spots. Booze was a powerful ally and scores of alcoholics believe that its powers directly benefited their upward climb in business and social circles. Another advantage to drinking was the self-esteem it afforded, the feeling any challenge could be met drink in hand. A measure of truth bolsters these beliefs. Alcohol is a depressant affecting the central nervous system. Consumed in small quantities, it may have the seemingly desirable ability to reduce feelings of inhibition. But that's all subject to change. In order to reclaim those early feelings of power, the alcoholic must consume more in an ongoing effort to meet his changing tolerance levels. Inhibitions relax to a degree that permits increasingly uncontrolled inappropriate behaviors. Even in this transitional stage, the alcoholic still believes the benefits of drinking more than compensate for the negative costs. As unpleasant as this stage may be, it only gets worse, for just ahead is the descent into alcohol addiction. The *need* for alcohol has now replaced its perceived fun and beneficial aspects. Alcohol has become the means to function in the everyday world. Now it is sobriety that doesn't feel natural. The urge to drink is uncontrollable. Excuse-making and deception skills are honed to better deflect questions of personal responsibility.

Another danger lies in wait; those who are addicted to alcohol have a greatly increased susceptibility for picking up additional addictions. As alcoholics move into the later stages, a creeping, slightly irrational awareness sets in, whereby the alcoholics begin to recognize that their good friend, the drink, has somehow let them down and turned its back on them. Gone are the days when a drink would ride to the rescue. The illusion of the enchanting elixir has vanished, only to be replaced by anger and hopelessness. Friends and co-workers have distanced themselves from the continuing emotional carnage. The likelihood of maintaining current employment or finding a new job is rapidly disappearing. Soon the alcoholic will enter into the disease's insidious final stage where misery and desperation is the web of life. The alcoholic's health erodes. Physical signs of the disease are increasingly apparent. Life has lost meaning, and the only form of relief seems to be in death. Suicide is now a realistic consideration. These developmental stages are played out more or less in a similar fashion for the majority of alcoholics. In most cases the stages are, at least in part, viewable by the public.

The Return of the Narcissist

The narcissist is addicted to recognition and adoration. Because the presence of one addictive behavior greatly increases the probability of acquiring another, alcoholism is not uncommon in the narcissist. For the narcissist, alcohol is a potent and accessible aid in keeping the real self hidden while increasing the larger than life aspects of the projected image. In the most negative of ways, the narcissistic condition and alcoholism seem to complement each other.

No venue supports the advancement of both narcissism and alcoholism better than the barroom. Here, the narcissist's all-important social status is acknowledged in a number of ways. Tokens of admiration, in the form of drinks, are purchased for him, and the people gather around. As time and liquor continue to flow, the limits of accepted social behavior expand. Feelings of admiration and friendship intensify and are displayed. Very rarely is anyone present in this setting to offer the narcissist criticism on any topic, least of all for excessive drinking. As the out-of-proportion show of approval carries on and narcissists receive their dose of recognition, their real self remains well guarded and safe. The superficiality of barroom relationships exposes nothing for which one would have to later account.

The alcoholic narcissist's chances of recovery are limited. To accept and admit the disease is to confess a failure of the false self and thereby expose the real self. He is painfully aware that the long-obscured fears of inadequacy and abandonment would likely be laid bare in the process of alcohol treatment. In the view of the narcissist, it would be better to remain an alcoholic than to take such a risk.

Alcoholism and Doctors

Alcoholism displays no deference to those of higher social status. In the medical profession, overworked physicians rationalize the hard use of alcohol while maintaining the belief that as doctors they are somehow immune to alcoholism.

These rationalizations and beliefs are gained early. In medical school the overwork begins, leaving the student little time to relax. What time there is for relaxation is fleeting, so one must learn to seize the moment and wring out of it all the available fun. Nothing can accelerate this process like alcohol. The problem with this quick fix philosophy is it assumes that, eventually, the level of stress will be abated and the need for instant relief will decline. But what if the stress does not significantly diminish, or it increases? Due to a change in tolerance levels, the alcohol-induced relaxing mini-vacation is not as effective as it once was, so the self-medication must be increased. And so begins the developmental stages of alcoholism.

How the onset of alcoholism would escape a medical doctor armed with a lofty education and an understanding of disease seems unfathomable, but it is probably for those very reasons that the disease is missed. Doctors place an enormous trust in their education, and from that trust grows a sense of invincibility in regard to the use of addictive drugs. They easily rationalize that alcoholism can't occur in trained, informed professionals. But that training, in addition to providing a false sense of security, may also contribute to the development of the disease in another subtle way. As medical students, doctors-to-be are instructed in the use of drugs designed to alleviate human discomfort. The adage of better living through chemistry seems true in part, and makes valid the use of alcohol for medicinal purposes—keeping the patient, or in this case the doctor, comfortable.

It is worth noting the alcoholic physician's risk to the dangers of prescription drugs. Doctors have a five times greater likelihood of taking sedatives without an independent medical prescription than the average citizen. The doctor's constant proximity to drugs plays a significant role. This risk is not limited solely to the addition of another addiction; the effects of synergism are a potent danger as well. Synergism is the cooperating interaction of two substances that result in a greater effect than the sum total of the substance's singular effects.

Synergism occurs when drugs of the same classification, such as depressants, are simultaneously active in the body. The results of such a pairing are often wildly unpredictable. If, for instance, an individual who is accustomed to the effects of a single Valium mixes that drug with, say bourbon, which he is also accustomed to, the reasonable expectation for this combination might be that one drug plus one drug equals two drugs. But drugs do not usually interact as a team. Instead, they increase the effects in such a fashion that one and one no longer equals two. Now one and one will equal six, or perhaps even more. Imagine the results of a two and two combination, or a four and four. It adds up to overdosing, often resulting in bad experiences, and even tragedy.

The self-denial behaviors that many physicians employ to deal with stress and overwork are an added hindrance when it comes to self-diagnosing alcoholism. Further, the mindset that maintains, "I'm the doctor, not the patient," also postpones or prevents altogether the seeking of help. Friends or family who wish to intervene are usually at a distinct disadvantage educationally, socially, and financially. It is difficult, unless he has hit rock bottom, to tell a medical doctor that he is making a serious error with alcohol, when by all appearances he is more successful than the confronter. The answer to this dilemma might seem to be for doctors to intervene with doctors on a professional basis.

A Conflict of Interest

For many reasons, doctors have an interest in the general image and success of their colleagues. It is important to doctors that patients receive the very best possible care, no matter from whom they receive it, but naturally doctors are also concerned with preserving the integrity of the medical institution and protecting their profession from scandal that could undermine the public's faith. Scandal, including issues of alcoholism, not only tarnish the profession's image but may also lead to more onerous regulations and increased malpractice insurance costs. Such issues then, it would seem, should be best dealt with internally, confidentially, and discreetly.

But the effort of simultaneously controlling public information while attempting to confront the problem of alcoholism in the medical profession can be extremely challenging and sometimes not very effective in its results. In many ways, it goes against the grain. Doctoring is a reactive profession; people come to a doctor seeking help—rather than the physician looking for a patient to treat. Doctors, understandably, rely heavily on their training, and that training—especially during the era in which Dr. Hume studied—did not address issues of occupational stress or the addictive behaviors associated with overwork, alcoholism, or prescription drug addiction. It was an area in which most doctors were ill-equipped to practice. Doctors also have strong ethical concerns about confidentiality, and while these concerns would be met by keeping a colleague's alcoholism out of the public arena, it also tends to hamper the attempts of a self-governing medical board to investigate and hold group discussions in its efforts to expose, confront, and aid in the treatment of a fellow physician. In many cases the whole process further enables, at least for a time, the alcoholic doctor. Nurses and other doctors step in to cover for him with excuses or by picking up duties. Work schedules might even be altered in an attempt to take advantage of periods of anticipated sobriety. No one wants to see a doctor lose his license, so every effort is made to provide the addicted physician shelter from the consequences of his behavior. The working alcoholic doctor's performance will continue to suffer. He will be tardy and may sometimes miss appointments altogether. Recordkeeping will lose its timeliness and accuracy. Impairment will become more evident as will symptoms of withdrawal. Patients, sooner or later, will be put at risk. Clearly alcoholism is a problem and, if ignored, will not go away. Any doctor will tell you that.

7

Way Up North

Leaving Little to Chance

Once Dr. Hume made up his mind, there was little chance he would change it, including his decision to move to Alaska. But as confident as he was, he also knew it was a long way to go without some assurance he could earn a living in the territory and that adequate housing would be available for his family. To reduce the risk of a costly wasted venture, the doctor flew to Alaska to make a few inquiries. His destination was Anchorage, the territory's largest city with a population of approximately 62,000. Upon arrival, he planned to first concentrate on securing employment, then attempt to locate housing. Luckily he was able to accomplish both goals in one stop. Dr. Hume applied to work with Dr. Romig's Anchorage Medical and Surgical Clinic and was hired. When introduced to staff physicians, Dr. Asa Martin offered a rental apartment in the Martin Arms, a complex he owned on the corner of 3rd and Unga Streets. Dr. Hume agreed to rent the apartment. The mission had been accomplished; he rejoined his family in Texas with a job and housing in Alaska already lined up.

The Road Before Them

In 1956, the remoteness of Alaska was enough to give any traveler pause. General public perception was of an ice and snow covered wasteland with only a few igloos dotting the otherwise barren landscape. Of course, this wasn't an accurate vision, but that's the way it had been depicted since Alaska's purchase from the Russians in 1867. As a result, few travelers heading that far north knew what to expect.

Although there were several ways north, the Humes chose to drive the Alaska Highway. It was a narrow, dusty, unpaved road stretching across western Canada, varying tremendously in elevation, badly in need of guardrails, hard on tires, and inconsistently maintained. A few scattered roadhouses along the way offered fuel, food, and lodging, but they were prone to irregular hours and going out of business. Sometimes the roadhouses were open for meals and not lodging or vice versa. Sometimes they served meals and had lodging available, but had run out of fuel. Some were only open for summer business. Fall travelers were often surprised that a roadhouse they had depended on for services had already closed for the winter. If a motorist experienced a mechanical difficulty, he would most likely be stranded at a lodge for several days or, depending on the seriousness of the repair, even a week or more. Budgeting time, money, and safety on the Alaska Highway was a series of calculated risks.

Making ready for their trip, the Humes padded the gas tank of their Chevrolet to help absorb some of the punishment that would be dealt by the washboard-like driving surface of the highway. Thankfully, they didn't need to haul furniture as the Martin Arms apartment came fully furnished. They traveled light, taking only clothes and a few pots and pans. They packed the rest of their belongings into a trailer, which they planned to put into storage in Seattle. They said goodbye to friends and family. Given the distance involved, family members wondered if they would ever see the Humes again.

The doctor did almost all the driving. Myrt entertained the children by reading to them along the way. The Humes stored the trailer in Seattle and then made their way into Canada to visit with John Hume before taking the route north. Warned about the dusty conditions of the gravel highway, they taped up their luggage and even the car windows to reduce the impact of the dirt. Their taping efforts weren't enough—the amount of dust was hard to imagine. From the traffic, great clouds of choking powder reduced visibility and filtered its way into everything. At overnight stops, the children's hair was washed several times to remove dirt that had accumulated from merely riding in the car. They pushed northward from Dawson Creek in British Columbia, through Fort St. John, Fort Nelson, and then Muncho Lake, and on to Watson Lake in Yukon Territory. Each night they stopped for a night's sleep at a roadhouse where they found the accommodations widely varying. One such stop found them overnight in a rather rustic cabin heated by a woodstove. In the early morning hours the fire died out, causing the poorly insulated building to cool off quickly. Myrt awoke to a cold cabin, dressed, and went outside in search of kindling. Bringing what wood she could find inside to break it up into manageable pieces, she was joined by her husband in restarting the fire. Later the doctor walked over to the main cabin to acquire water. There he was told by the owner he shouldn't be walking around outside because of the presence of bears. Sometimes the roadhouse owners would inexplicably deny them lodging altogether, perhaps due to their large family. On one occasion while traveling late in the day in the higher elevations they encountered heavy sleet. The road conditions worsened, and they experienced some dreaded automobile troubles too. They stopped at a motel for the night, and were refused a room. Turned away, they traveled another 100 icy miles with the benefit of only one headlight and no taillights before finding a room to rent. In the following days, they passed through Whitehorse, Haines Junction, and Beaver Creek on their way to the Alaska-Canada border near Tok Junction. With 1,314 miles of the Alaska Highway behind them, they were once again on American soil.

The next leg of the trip was on the Glenn Highway heading west. This part of the journey took the Humes on a much improved paved highway extending from Glenallen past a number of lodges, sheep-dotted mountains, rivers, lakes, and a vast glacier to Palmer. From Palmer they continued south to Anchorage.

Anchorage, Air Crossroads of the World

Anchorage was a still a young city when the Humes arrived in late September of 1956. The city had been established as a result of the Alaska Railroad Bill signed by President Woodrow Wilson in 1914. The construction of an Alaska Railroad required a base of operation, and the Ship Creek area of what would become Anchorage seemed a natural choice. It had a fine location for the construction of a wharf, fresh water was available, and with the Matanuska Valley coalfields in proximity it had excellent potential to serve as a coal terminal. Over the next forty years, Anchorage experienced several more booms, including one related to national defense with the buildup in connection with World War II. Despite an economic cycle of boom and bust, an Alaska tradition, the city showed steady progress. By 1956 Anchorage boasted eleven schools, a bus service, two busy airports, two television stations, three radio stations, and two daily newspapers. There were four theaters, a golf course, a community chorus, and a symphony orchestra. The city contained two hospitals and miles of water, sanitary sewer, and storm drain lines. Many of the streets were paved and there were more than 1,300 street lights. Residents were proud of their city and never prouder than when Anchorage received "All American City" status for 1956 as proclaimed by the National Municipal League and *Look* magazine.

Myrt was impressed that Anchorage was a modern city. The city surpassed all her expectations. The Martin Arms apartment complex was a series of rectangular buildings containing as many as eight apartments to a building. Their apartment was a small two bedroom place, so small that Myrt found she could clean the entire apartment in an hour. After the long expensive trip over the Alaska Highway and the payment of first and last months' rent, the Humes had $4 remaining cash. With no money and no time to waste, Dr. Hume went to work at the clinic the very day after they arrived. After one week, the office manager asked Dr. Hume if he wanted to be paid right then or would rather wait until the next week. Not wanting to seem desperately in need of money, Dr. Hume casually replied that whatever was easiest for the office manager would suit him as well. The manager went ahead and paid him immediately, much to his and Myrt's relief.

The family began to adjust to their new circumstances. April, now six years old, began school in Anchorage. The doctor was off to work each morning. With only one car, this left Myrt somewhat apartment-bound. She felt particularly stuck because she was without her sewing machine, which had remained in storage in Seattle. For Myrt, the sewing machine was an important tool in her contribution to the family's economy as a means of offsetting clothing costs. The sewing machine was also her creative outlet and in many ways, her sanctuary.

Finally she rented a machine. It was good timing, for if she felt apartment-bound in the Alaska fall, the approaching winter could only be worse.

Their first Alaska winter was a challenge for the Humes. It was cold and there was a lot of snow. So much snow that the Chevrolet became hopelessly buried for awhile and the doctor was forced to take a cab to work. In the clutches of a harsh winter, with restricted mobility and still very little cash, the couple decided that Alaska may not have been the best choice for them after all. They decided to save what money they could in preparation for leaving. They thought they might give Oregon a try. They were serious enough about moving to Oregon that the doctor looked into the state's licensing requirements. He found Oregon had a medical license reciprocity agreement with Texas, similar to the one between Texas and Alaska. He had received his license to practice medicine in Alaska without further examination, but Oregon required physicians to pass one additional test before receiving their certificate. Dr. Hume flew to Oregon and took the test, which he passed, earning a license to practice medicine in that state as well. But when he returned to Alaska, he was not as anxious to move. Somehow his absence from the territory had made his heart grow fonder for the place, as if Alaska was better appreciated from the outside looking in.

Whatever his motivations, he suggested to Myrt that they stay in Alaska and she agreed. They also decided to upgrade their accommodations. They found an affordable small two story, three bedroom house in the Lake Otis area. The upstairs was unfinished and unusable, and it was small enough that the dining room table was situated in the living room, but a house was an improvement over an apartment and they purchased it. With the coming school year, April was enrolled in the second grade, with Dawn attending first grade at Lake Otis Elementary. Despite all this forward momentum, the doctor was still not altogether happy with the family's standard of living or his professional pursuits. In the summer of 1958, he was searching for something more. He wanted to open a private practice and he wanted to live outside the Anchorage area, perhaps in a place like that small town, Palmer, they had passed through on the way to Anchorage. Myrt, a small town girl at heart, concurred.

8

The Road to Palmer

Motoring North

Their route north took the Humes across town through the Mountain View district of Anchorage out onto what was then known as the Palmer Highway. The road to Palmer roughly paralleled the path of the Alaska Railroad. The Palmer Highway accommodated no high speed trips. Although its surface was asphalt, the road was narrow without benefit of shoulders. In places, seasonal frost heaving gave the ride a roller coaster effect. In areas of extreme heaving, pavement breaks appeared. It was a highway of many curves and few guardrails. The trip took the Humes through a number of small settlements as the road skirted the base of the Chugach Mountains. They drove through the town of Eagle River and passed above Fire Lake while the road increased in elevation. Shortly they were offered great vistas of Knik Arm and, in the distance, North America's highest peak, Mount McKinley. They drove by a number of roadhouses including the popular Spring Creek Lodge owned by Vernon and Alma Haik. The highway lost elevation as it passed through Chugiak and proceeded into the Birchwood and Mirror Lake areas. Next came Eklutna Village, with its old log Russian Orthodox church, a local landmark. Beyond the village was the Eklutna Flats, with an array of wildflowers including shooting stars of pink and gold and the Alaska wild iris, colored in violet and blue. Here the highway and the railroad took separate paths. At the Knik River, the Alaska Railroad continued its northerly route and traversed the Knik and Matanuska Rivers over several bridges. The highway turned east, fitting tightly between the Knik River and the base of Pioneer Peak. This was a lonely stretch of highway shrouded in the shadow of the peak that rose sharply above it. It was an area of active avalanche movement in the late winter and early spring. Another hazard in this section of the highway occurred when Lake George, a high lake between mountain and glacier, broke through its retaining ice dam to flood the Knik River bed and the highway below. Fortunately, those perils did not manifest themselves during the Humes' trip; they continued on, passing by the Knik Drive Inn, "Home of the Husky Burger," veering left and proceeding north again to the approach of the Knik River bridge.

The Community Center under construction. (*Neal Wright family collection*)

The Community Center

More than twenty years earlier, in 1936, the Knik River bridge had been completed, opening a vital transportation link between the colony and Anchorage. For the Matanuska Valley, it was a time of unprecedented construction. In the community's center, where construction had begun in 1935, work continued the following year and with it the completion of Central School a massive, lap sided, three story building measuring 57 feet by 135 feet. The new colony school sported a gymnasium complete with a stage and balcony seating. The gymnasium was used for a multitude of community gatherings from governmental to recreational. The majority of the community's structures were nearly complete by this time, including a water tower, warehouse, hatchery, poultry house, creamery, and powerhouse. The administration building was finished, as was the garage, trading post, teachers' dormitories, and several churches. As for the colonists, nearly all had taken occupancy in their new homes just prior to the coming of their first winter in the valley.

The Elements

Close observance of the Matanuska Valley's weather was a principal requirement in any new resident's continuing education. The location, terrain, and other environmental factors so dramatically affected the climate that the valley was beyond the realm of experience for most newcomers. The region's high latitude bestowed summer days with extended hours of daylight. The ice fields and their glacier-fed rivers provided a cooling influence, as did the semi-coastal location, which contributed to moderate temperatures. But this same high latitude was also responsible for the length of the summer, which was decidedly short. For this reason there was certain urgency to the season—a prevailing sense of limited time for construction, subsistence-related activities, and for fun in the sun. Signs of winter came early, beginning as early as July with the summer rains. The rain was welcomed initially as a reprieve from a dry spring and early summer. But the welcome didn't last because sometimes the rain continued for weeks, causing construction, farm work, and other important tasks to slow at a critical juncture right before the onset of fall, which could arrive suddenly.

With fall, the beautiful and abundant fireweed plants, which could grow as tall as six feet, lost their bright crimson flowers and went to seed in a white flurry—foretelling the coming snow. The advancement of snow down the mountains was then eyed warily by the residents. The days became shorter and, of course, colder. Winter usually, but by no means always, came in November. It might begin earlier or after several false starts it might settle in later. When winter did arrive to stay, it generally could be categorized as moderately cold with relatively light snowfall. Warm chinook winds, sometimes accompanied by mid-winter rain, were not unusual. These warm spells generally caused more harm than good because water from melting ice and snow had no place to go and found its way into basements or caused "glaciating" under roofing material, resulting in leaks. The excess water was also a problem in transportation when sheets of glare ice formed with the next inevitable freeze cycle. The winter winds were the most violent aspect of a valley winter. The winds, with high-strength gusts, closed roads with drifting snow, damaged buildings, and caused the wind-chill factor to plummet, creating a risk to human safety. But the only predictable aspect of winter was the greatly reduced hours of sunlight. For months, the sun appeared for only five or six hours a day. Winter light deprivation was a basic element of what the old-timers referred to as "cabin fever," a malady similar to depression. Spring always brought hope, nowhere more so than Alaska. The Matanuska Valley usually enjoyed clear spring days, and those who drew livelihood from the land anxiously anticipated the thawing soils and the warmth that would nourish their crops. For the colonists, the weather was but another challenge in a long list of challenges.

The Colony Revisited

After that first winter, and with spring upon the Matanuska Valley, the colony farmers found themselves already behind schedule. The timetable had slipped the previous year when home construction had proceeded much slower than anticipated. In an attempt to accelerate the building program, some of the land clearing efforts had slowed. The timetable for farmers to start producing enough food for their own consumption and selling the surplus looked as if it may be delayed for a year, resulting in another year of unplanned costs and more extended credit for the colonists.

The colonists were used to being poor, but that didn't mean they liked it. They felt they should have been doing better, but things beyond their control were holding them back. These feelings gave rise to a mighty frustration. It was increasingly apparent during the clearing and tilling process that the forty-acre tracts were not large enough for their intended purpose. Few of the tracts were 100 percent tillable, reducing the amount of farmable land. Many farms held fewer than twenty acres of useable farm land. Even if all forty acres were completely tillable, some wondered if that would be enough for a successful subsistence farm. But the colonists toiled on.

While work on the farms continued, the program's administrative branch established the Matanuska Valley Farmer's Cooperative Association. The Co-op's purpose was, in part, to buy and sell the colonists' surplus farm produce. The Co-op also sold household staples and other items not manufactured locally. But the Co-op carried a stipulation. Membership in the association was mandatory, as was the sale of any farm surpluses. Not only were the colonists required to buy and sell through the Co-op, so were any successive owners of their colony property. When the farms began to produce enough to sell, the farmers were dismayed at the low price the Co-op offered. In short order it became obvious that the long days and short summer offered prodigious crop harvests, but little crop variety. Everyone was raising the same crops. A number of colonists began to look for a market for their produce elsewhere in the territory. This was a breach of their Co-op agreement. The breaches led to official reprimands and eventually lawsuits.

Four years after its optimistic beginnings, more than sixty percent of the original families had abandoned the colony program, for a number of reasons, and left the valley. The abandoned land tracts were often combined with existing working farms in an effort to make those farms a sustaining enterprise. Replacement colonists were recruited for several more years with a refined selection process to better screen for qualified applicants. Also, in the following years a number of the program's more onerous regulations and restrictions were discontinued, lessening some of the colonists' frustrations. But their high debt remained and that alone was cause for worry.

For a great many in the colony, the military buildup associated with the Second World War was a boon to their financial survival. For the first time, military base construction near Anchorage brought good, high paying jobs to the region. Colony men claimed a number of those jobs, living and working in Anchorage during the week and returning home as their work schedule permitted. During this period, the women and children worked the farms. The buildup had another, longer lasting benefit for the farmers. Servicemen, stationed at the bases, provided a new, large consumer center for valley produce. As the military bases grew, so grew the surrounding infrastructure and population of Anchorage—and more people meant more food was needed. The focus on vegetable farming shifted to include dairy operations and the resulting agricultural diversity met with success. In addition to these positive events, the colonists now had control of the administration of their colony. The challenges continued, but at least now the colony was a self-governing entity.

Progress

For early residents of the Matanuska Valley, the advances of the 1940s and 1950s must have seemed unimaginable. Under the Rural Electrification Administration another cooperative was born, the Matanuska Electric Association. MEA brought electricity to 150 customers in 1942 and continued a rapid expansion of its facilities and service area. A public library opened in Palmer, and a new local newspaper went into print. Banking was established with the founding of Matanuska Valley Bank. Additional banking services soon became available with the creation of the Matanuska Valley Federal Credit Union. In 1951, Palmer incorporated as a first class city. Two years earlier, the United States Department of Agriculture (USDA) had opened a branch in Palmer. Matanuska Telephone Association was founded to meet the area's communication needs. In 1958, Palmer's main streets received an asphalt surface. Much had been accomplished from such humble beginnings. The benefits of this progress, however, were not uniformly enjoyed.

Homesteading

Homesteading had long since come to an end in the contiguous states, leaving Alaska as the lone area with federal land still available. Just as the colonists had done years earlier, homesteaders journeyed north in the 1950s, with expectations of a fresh start. If colonizing was difficult, then homesteading was positively grim. It started with a hopeful applicant who was in most cases severely under-capitalized, filing on marginal land well outside the developing community. Some of the parcels were so remote that the road system had not yet reached the area. In such cases, the homesteaders were forced to drive as far as the available roads would take them, then begin walking or traveling by railroad, to reach their land. The provisions for homesteading included goals that, if met, would ultimately lead to parcel ownership. Among the goals to be "proved up" were the construction of a domicile, the clearing of a given amount of land, and the establishment of a crop. The homestead also had to be occupied for a specified number of months each year. Because money was impossibly scarce, the house was often little more than a small poorly insulated log or frame tar-paper box heated with a fifty-five gallon drum fashioned into a woodstove. Utilities were not available, so water was either hauled in or fetched from a nearby stream. Indoor plumbing did not exist, so outdoor privies were the norm. Lighting was by kerosene lamps or Blazo fuel lanterns. The wooden boxes the Blazo tins were shipped in were sometimes fashioned into rudimentary cupboards and shelving. Homesteaders learned to make do with what they had.

The hitch to proving up a homestead was that the land was years away from providing any substantial level of subsistence living, which forced the applicant off the parcel in search of work elsewhere. And, if the homesteaders were not available to clear land, plant and tend a crop, or even occupy the home-stead, they had failed to meet the goals set forth for obtaining a title. Homesteading was a frustrating proposition. In spite of this, the homesteading program continued to draw applicants, who would face almost the identical trials of their predecessors, into the 1960s.

The City Limits

As the Humes crossed the Knik River bridge and back onto the blacktop, they proceeded toward the Bodenburg Loop area of the Matanuska Valley. On the left they passed Delroi's, a bar and restaurant renown for tasty barbecue food. Just ahead, rising almost 650 feet out of the adjacent farmland was "The Butte." A little farther on the right was Barnhardt's Sawmill. Past a few more twists and turns, the Palmer Highway opened up a bit to a long straightaway which closely paralleled Bodenburg Creek where large, brightly-colored salmon could be seen during spawning season. Down's Market, a small neighborhood grocery store, lay ahead. Shortly, the highway returned to twists and turns, passing by Lazy Mountain ascending to the right. The Matanuska River bridge was ahead. Beyond the bridge, they neared the city limits, and after passing the local cemetery, the Humes reached their destination—the city of Palmer.

In 1958, Palmer still retained much of the look of a government town. East of the railroad tracks was the town center, a number of buildings of similar appearance, the vision of the early colonization architects and planners. West of the tracks, the private business district occupied buildings of varied architectural style. Private dwellings varied in design as well, except in a small housing development on the northwest side of town and the tract housing for employees of the Experimental Station in a section of southeast Palmer.

The main street in Palmer, shortly before the Hume's arrival. (*Ward Wells photographer, Anchorage Museum at Rasmuson Center*)

The Businesses

The Humes found the private businesses, coupled with the services of the Co-op, made Palmer a surprisingly self-sufficient community. Those in search of men's clothing could shop at the Co-op Trading Post or at Koslosky's Department Store. Women's clothing could be purchased at Betty's and the Trading Post. Automobiles were available through Hartley Motors, Kirk's Sales & Service, and Everett Motor. A number of choices were available for auto service and repair, among them Westside Service, Norm's Super Service, Tost's Service, and Pioneer Texaco. Lodging options included the Hyland Hotel and the Matanuska Hotel which sported forty-two rooms and forty-two baths. Hardware could be purchased at the Co-op and Reed's Hardware & Sporting Goods. Building supplies were available at the Palmer location of Ketchikan Spruce Mills. Prescription drugs could be obtained from Bert's Drugstore and the Palmer Drugstore. For groceries there were several choices: Koslosky's, Piggly-Wiggly Super Market, and the smaller North Palmer Store. There were even places for recreation too—The

Valley Theatre, which was soon to be remodeled and called The Center Theatre, and a bowling alley, The Palmer Bowling Center, later known as the D'Gutter. The town had a travel agency, flower shops, and dry cleaners. Farm equipment was available through the Co-op and, for John Deere products, Brook's Equipment Company. Several eating establishments were present, including the coffee shop at the Matanuska Hotel, the Palmer Café, and the Maranda Café. Bert's Drugstore also had a lunch counter. Plumbing services were available from either Mac's or Withey Plumbing & Heating. Insurance needs could be met through the Pippel or Woods Insurance Agencies. The Co-op had a machine shop, as did Goodrich's Palmer Machinery across from the high school. Palmer had a bakery, variety store, auto parts stores, a body and paint shop, and a funeral chapel. Services were provided by attorneys, barbers, and women's hair stylists. Two Anchorage television stations served Palmer, KTVA Channel 11 and KENI Channel 2. A television could be purchased or repaired through Alaska TV Sales & Service. The goods and services available were surprisingly plentiful and varied for a far north frontier town. This was especially true if one imbibed in alcoholic beverages. If a person needed a drink, he had indeed come to the right place.

The members-and-guests-only Elks and Moose Lodges each had a club that served drinks. These two establishments had strict codes of conduct. The use of offensive language, belligerent, or inappropriate behavior was not tolerated. The other bars, which were open to the public in Palmer, were more relaxed in their expectations. The Shamrock Lounge was a prime example. The Shamrock, located in the northern portion of the business district on Palmer's main street, had a modest décor save for the curved bar reminiscent of a clover leaf. Besides drinking, some kind of physical activity or contest always seemed to be going on at the Shamrock. Patrons engaged in "Indian leg wrestling," arm wrestling, or finger-pulling, where two contestants hooked middle fingers and pulled in an attempt to straighten the opponent's finger, thereby defeating him. Once, when a traveling rodeo came to town, a bucking pony was brought into the Shamrock for the patrons to ride.

The antithesis of the Shamrock, just up the street, was the sleepy bar at the Matanuska Hotel which catered mainly to hotel guests. A little south of the Shamrock, at the northwest quadrant of Palmer's four-way intersection was Steve and Sally Ward's Frontier Bar. Across the street and down a narrow concrete sidewalk, past the Variety Store, was the Tropical Gardens owned by Bill and Ruby Miller. The Tropical Gardens featured the flavor of the South Seas, resplendently decorated with painted rocks, fish tanks and green tinsel fashioned to appear as island flora. Next door, the neon sign on the 49 Club's log façade proclaimed that "Floor Shows" were performed inside. Down the street from the 49 Club, past the barber shop, the Piggly Wiggly, Betty's, the bank, and Ray's Liquor Store, was Bob and Ruth Peterson's Palmer Bar located in the basement of Bert's Drugstore. Not all the bars in the Matanuska Valley were located in Palmer. Green Acres, approximately ten miles out of Palmer on Wasilla Lake was a popular destination, as was Phil and Jean O'Neill's Alpine Inn at Sutton, which did a brisk business serving the crews working in the nearby coal mines. A number of other watering holes existed as well, sprinkled around the Butte area, Wasilla, and Big Lake, but for the sheer number of taverns concentrated in a small area, Palmer surpassed them all. None of the bars suffered from a lack of business.

The Frontier Lifestyle

Palmer was a hard drinking town. People liked to say of a night of partying, "We started at the north end and worked our way to the south end." Bar events were called "functions" and there was one every Saturday night. If the party went long, then normal business hours were overlooked. Often, the bars did not close at all, since somebody was always in need of a drink. The revelry of an active social scene was not all the taverns had to offer. Games of chance were available too, with several establishments furnishing tables for stakes card games. Little effort was made to conceal the betting. Business was conducted at the pubs too, and lots of it. Deals were struck in the better bars with a toast of a glass. Loans were often previewed verbally, over a few drinks with local lenders assessing the loan's viability before proceeding with any official paperwork. Sometimes the paperwork was nothing more than a formality, as loan approval had already been granted at a local tavern.

Several factors help explain why alcohol was consumed with such regularity and in such volume, and why so much legitimate, as well as illegitimate, activity occurred openly. The frontier population was anything but static. Most of the residents were from someplace else, having recently relocated to the area. The largely transient population had few of the encumbrances or inhibitions that come with established roots in a community. Many of the migratory residents had journeyed north specifically to avoid some of the rules of social behavior observed in the States. And the Matanuska Valley had a young population. Approximately eighty-two percent of the area's inhabitants were under forty-five years of age. Young people tend to party harder and in engage in riskier behavior than their elders. The context of the times is also vital in understanding the behaviors associated with heavy drinking in the territorial Matanuska Valley. Behavior which would be considered inappropriate today, such as driving with an open container, was not regarded so then. Even driving while intoxicated carried little of the social stigma that it does today. The legal consequences for drunken driving were not as great. If a motorist had too much to drink and was pulled over by the police, the driver was far more likely to be escorted home, given a ride home in the patrol car, or allowed to make another arrangement for transportation than to be taken into custody. Not all of the area's residents misused alcohol—many consumed moderately or not at all. But remote, untamed frontier towns have historically seen high rates in alcohol abuse, and Palmer was no different.

The people of the valley shared a real, almost palpable, sense of camaraderie. People were expected to do for themselves, to be sure, but people were quick to help others, too. Folks would often toil harder in an effort to help friends and neighbors than they would for themselves. Motorists rarely passed by someone broken down or stranded by the road. People were friendly—they waved, made eye contact, said hello, and everybody knew everybody. It was no utopia, and not everyone liked everyone else, but maybe people just felt a little more grateful to have each other. The place had its share of colorful characters, and raw individualism was accepted, if not prized, but somehow it all contributed to a spirit of community, one of inclusion, where volunteerism ran high. People showed up for things and took an interest. They attended high school sporting events whether or not they had children participating. They attended meetings. Most felt certain that if they worked together, everyone would benefit.

Palmer residents may have been of a single purpose, but were not always of one mind. Huge public rows took place when differing viewpoints clashed. During such conflicts, length of residency was usually equated with superior knowledge and vision. Many proclamations began with, "I've been here since (-insert year here-) and I say..." in a classic show of frontier one-upmanship. And despite the camaraderie, a fair number of cliques developed, most often, again, based on length of residency. The early settlers cast a wary eye on those newcomers, the colonists. The colonists generally viewed the replacement colonists as Johnny-come-latelys, and the pre-war residents had less respect for the postwar residents. The newly-arrived homesteaders also endured a period on the outside looking in. The frontier lifestyle eventually rounded off some of the sharper edges, especially when times were hard, the chips were down, and the residents' struggles were shared.

Any class or social distinction was lost with the quest for winter provisions. One might find himself pulling a salmon set net at Fish Creek with a day laborer on one side and an attorney on the other. Everyone depended on having fish and moose meat in the freezer. Virtually every family had a garden. Local produce and dairy products were fresh and plentiful. Folks picked berries: wild raspberries, salmonberries, currants, and low and highbush cranberries for use in jam, jellies, and pie. It didn't take much of a green thumb to raise rhubarb, which was used in a number of dessert dishes, but most of all in pie. The local fresh, fresh frozen, or home canned food was almost always of superior quality to food brought in from Outside. Imported food, most of which came by boat, was generally poor. Fruit, which was picked green for easier handling, arrived bruised and still hard after the long journey. The shipped-in food was stale-tasting, which gave rise to the notion among the locals that if food went unsold in Lower 48 stores and was on the shelf past its prime, it was removed and shipped to Alaska. All imported food was costly—roughly thirty-five percent higher than in other west coast states.

In some ways, day-to-day life in Palmer was much the same as anywhere else in the United States—adults worked and kids went to school or enjoyed the freedom of summer vacation. Most of the women worked at home, and those employed elsewhere usually worked in offices or in retail stores. A large portion of the adult men were engaged in some form of seasonal construction trade, or in farming. Such seasonal activities called for long hours, six or seven days a week, during the short summer and fall seasons. Those who had steady occupations in town usually pulled a more even strain. For most of these employees, the work day was signaled by the Co-op's four whistle blows, at 8 A.M, noon, 1 P.M. and 5 P.M.

The children of these workers were a largely independent bunch. Many grew up walking some distance to school or the bus stop in winter darkness and inclement weather while watching for dangerously protective cow moose with calves. The general impression was that kids could get into little real trouble, so parents usually allowed children great autonomy. Youngsters had lots of woods and fields to play in and could have fun with activities such as sledding and skiing. Little League baseball was the summer team sport for boys. Many kids had access to firearms, which they used for target practice and hunting. The local streams, rivers, and lakes afforded ample fishing. Summer jobs for teens were most often found on farms—weeding and picking produce or bucking hay bales. Kids also bagged and carried groceries or waited and bussed tables in local eateries.

The education available to these young people was surprisingly advanced for a town on the frontier or, for that matter, anywhere else. Good educators were teaching in a community environment that promoted the value of an education. This positive approach was no doubt influenced, in part, by the personnel employed by the USDA in Palmer. This was a group of highly educated people who had high expectations of the school system and of their own and other children within that system. They were willing to be involved, as were others, and all the children benefited. Educational facilities in Palmer included the massive Central School, constructed during colonization, that housed grades one through eight, and the newer Palmer High School. As the Humes were pulling into town, planning was in the latter stages for an expansion to Swanson Elementary School, which would soon handle grades one through four.

In Palmer, one could come face-to-face with living history. For instance, by talking to local residents who had actually taken part in the Gold Rush, one could hear a firsthand account of history that was unavailable anywhere in the contiguous states. Plenty of folks were still around who could recall a time before the railroad ran in the vicinity, or who remembered when white settlements in the area were first being built. It was all part of the romanticism of living on the frontier, where one could blaze an original trail or talk to a person who had. Because people who moved to the area were forced to travel light, few personal possessions could be characterized as heirlooms or antiques. Everything was new.

Palmer had some of the elements of Andy Griffith's Mayberry. Almost everybody shared a telephone party line and was subjected to long waits while fellow party liners tied up the phone. Often a resident would hear another phone pick up during their conversation—privacy was never assured. Kids couldn't get away with skipping school or similar mischief because in an everybody-knows-everybody town, word always got back to their parents. Along with hard news stories, the local newspaper—*The Frontiersman*—also ran short features on subjects such as how a woman might best get in and out of modern low automobiles. *The Frontiersman* also ran front page pieces on who was leaving town on vacation, where they were going, and how long they would be gone. Children's birthday party reports, including guest lists, were also featured on the front page. When the Humes arrived, the Palmer Police Department was still four years away from having its own telephone number.

The town had an underbelly too, as does every community. Much of the worst of it was connected with the abuse of alcohol, which was largely out in the open. But there were other matters too, matters far more private, such as abortions and paperless adoptions. Anchorage had come to think of itself as all grown-up and civilized, where certain matters would draw undue attention. It was therefore considered prudent to move unsavory matters out of Anchorage and push them north to a place where discretion would be better observed. Palmer was the place to get such things done.

Politically, the area leaned toward the democratic ticket in voting habits. However, one issue galvanized and united Democrats and Republicans alike the summer the Humes arrived in Palmer. It was the prospect of statehood. Statehood was advertised, in part, as an opportunity to play a larger role in self-government and to receive a greater portion of the federal dollar. It was looked upon as an issue of progress and the residents wanted progress. The Statehood Referendum passed by a wide margin.

The Leaders

The politicians elected to represent the interests of the citizenry are only a part of the leadership in a community. Numerous other individuals serving on various boards and councils, for organizations that are both nonprofit and for profit, are important components of an area's leadership. Palmer in 1958 had all of those, and others as well—others who didn't fit the conventional mold of community leader. In that place and time, an individual could exert real control and leadership in the community by the sheer force of personality. Some individuals in Palmer assumed leadership roles due, in part, to their education or their vocation. Such leaders included Alvin DeJulio, publisher of *The Frontiersman* newspaper; Allan Mick, Director of the Experimental Station; Dick Jones in banking; and Jan Koslosky, store owner, banker and later elected politician, to name a few. But there was another kind of leader who eschewed the limelight and didn't run for elective office; the type of person content with working behind the scenes exercising his own brand of control and leadership. Such an individual was Neal Wright.

Neal

Wright was born Joseph Kowal in Snohomish, Washington in the late summer of 1905 to an affluent family of German descent. His father worked as a railroad contractor. Wright's mother passed away when he was about seven. Wright was raised Catholic but soon turned away from the church when, at the age of ten, as he was sitting in a pew looking back to see the people seated behind him, a woman brought her umbrella down hard upon his head. The negative attention humiliated him. He always associated this experience with the church and did not return. He grew into a young man with curly black hair and sharp blue eyes. Wright stood above average in height with a medium build. He was a friendly person and exercised a great sense of humor, sometimes in a bawdy vein. Billiards was a favorite pastime. He was very intelligent. He pursued an education in medicine with the financial support of his father. As an undergraduate he attended Washington State College; later he graduated from Northwestern University Medical School. He had planned to become a doctor, but late in his last year of school he altered his course of study to become a pharmacist. It proved to be a wise choice in matters of quality of life. The work hours of a pharmacist were far superior to that of an on-call physician.

The years between Wright's graduation and his marriage became the stuff of small town legend, filled with stories of his dealings with Al Capone and various mob types while residing in gangland Chicago. The stories may or may not have been true, but in any case, the joker Wright made little effort to dispel them. Wright journeyed north in 1932, entering the territory of Alaska through Seward with a final destination of Anchorage. When he entered into marriage with Marie Anderson, he drew the ire of his father who disapproved of his choice in a wife. Neal and Marie wanted to make a fresh start on their own, so they returned to frontier Alaska. The Wrights worked hard in a variety of jobs. At first, to make ends meet Neal took jobs as a taxi driver, an electrician, and a radio repairman. Later Neal worked as a doctor's assistant in a hospital operating room. His knowledge of the latest operating protocols was sometimes greater than the physicians he was assisting. On more than one occasion, he performed almost an entire procedure when the doctor of record was impaired by drink. While working as a doctor's assistant, he also worked as a pharmacist for Z.J. Loussac. The Wright's savings, meager upon arrival, grew steadily. Soon they had an opportunity to purchase an interest in a drugstore. The Wrights entered into business with Osky Weeda in the Anchorage pharmacy, Bert's Drugstore, named for Osky's brother. When the opportunity became available to expand the business to the developing colony project in Palmer, Osky and Neal flipped a coin to determine which would venture north and open the new business. Neal won the toss.

Neal and Marie moved to Palmer and lived directly behind Bert's Drugstore, with only a narrow alley separating the home and business. The Wrights soon bought full interest in the store. The townspeople found their new druggist to be a generous man who regularly provided medicine to those who couldn't pay. Pharmacists have a traditional role as lower level health-care providers, giving treatment advice along with prescription and over-the-counter medicines. This pharmacist, the residents found, was willing to take on much greater responsibility. Neal would dispense drugs, in emergency situations, without a doctor's written prescription. He would do what he felt he had to. The new pharmacist was generous in other ways too. He took people under his wing. He gave charitably, often, and anonymously. He mixed well with everyone and seemed blind to the conventions of social status. He liked to drink, and he minded his own business. He was no saint and everyone knew and accepted it. The drugstore prospered under Neal's ownership. His investments in other businesses and the stock market made him a wealthy man. After a fire in the late 1940s burned the store to the ground, the Wrights rebuilt at the same location. The new building was quite large with upstairs and basement space for rent. The ground floor housed the pharmacy, general merchandise sales, the Palmer Post Office, a lunch counter, a travel agency, and a barber shop. The drugstore carried merchandise in a wide range of prices. Additionally, Neal would special order anything his customers desired outside the customary drugstore wares. Dishes, carpet, appliances—whatever was needed, Neal could get. His drugstore was the primary meeting spot in downtown Palmer. By the summer of 1958, the drugstore staff included another pharmacist, Tatso Gosho whom everyone called "Tats," and clerks Deb Anderson, Bud Campbell, and Ruth Peterson. Henry Liebing handled the jewelry counter. Neal worked in the pharmacy, and Marie managed the lunch counter.

Neal was by now a member of the old guard, an established businessman and leader. He still avoided public attention but could be counted on for advice if asked. His hair was turning white by then, and his medium build had thickened, giving him a solid appearance. He remained generous and was still a bit of a rascal. His sense of humor was well intact. With the arrival of the Humes, Neal gained a friendship with Myrt and a professional association and deep friendship with Dr. Hume with whom he shared much in common.

9

Home at Last

A Very Fine House

The Hume's house hunting in Palmer coincided perfectly with the marketing of Don Mealy's home at the north end of Matanuska Street. The house suited the Hume's many needs. It featured a full, twenty-eight by thirty-seven foot concrete block basement that could be converted into the doctor's of-

The Hume's home and office. (*Cheryl Homme*)

fice. The main floor, while not overly spacious, was comfortably sized. It even had a small attic. The midtown location was good, and the house's exterior appearance made it a local

117

landmark. It was a beautiful log home that was so well-maintained the logs glistened. A great flat gray-colored block chimney offset and complemented the deep luster of the golden wood. It was the very model of a modern Alaska log house. In the style of the dwelling, an attractive twenty-nine by twenty foot two-car log garage stood at the corner of the lot. No house in Palmer was like it. Rather extensive interior remodeling was needed, but the Humes loved it. They bought the house and put their Anchorage home up for sale.

They had much to do. The family's new first floor living space was essentially a two-bedroom situation, making for tight sleeping quarters for two adults and four children. To remedy this lack of bedroom space, the Humes had work done in the unused and unfinished attic. First, access to the attic was established with the construction of a stairway. Only a portion of the attic was floored, an area measuring approximately twelve by twenty-two feet. The part of the attic that was to remain unfinished was separated from the bedroom area with a new interior wall. A window was cut into the logs, allowing some natural lighting in the new bedroom and also to serve as an emergency exit. The staircase leading to the attic was so narrow and steep that conventional beds and dressers would not fit through the opening. Even if they had, the attic's ceiling, which followed the sharp pitch of the roof and was only five feet ten inches at the tallest center point, did not allow for the placement of furniture directly against the walls. To solve this problem, the Humes hired a carpenter to build in dressers conforming to the pitch of the ceiling, against one exterior wall. Three metal Army cot frames were purchased from Johnny's Surplus Store and shortened in length. Mattresses for the cots were cut to fit the frames. The cots were placed end to end against the exterior wall opposite the built-in dressers and stairway opening. This would be the bedroom for April, Dawn, and Cindy.

The main floor required the least amount of work. The back door to the house opened in to a small landing, with a few stairs on the left leading to the main floor. A door at the top of this short flight of stairs led immediately into the kitchen. The kitchen had ample room and benefited from a large rectangular window above the sink, offering mountain views. Off the kitchen was the living room, featuring a large stone fireplace, and to the left was the dining area. Both the living and dining rooms were enhanced by a number of large windows. A hallway to the right of the kitchen led to Frank's bedroom and the master bedroom, both on the left. At the end of the hallway was the bathroom. The hallway also contained the attic stairway. It wasn't by any means a small house, but the perceived size of a building is relative to the number of inhabitants, and soon the Hume house would have another. Myrt was going to have a baby.

A Home Office

As expensive as the home renovations were, they could not compare with the funds required for setting up an office and buying the necessary medical equipment. For the Humes this was particularly troubling because the expected infusion of cash from the sale of their Anchorage home had not materialized. Instead they were left with two house payments and the prospects of a limited cash flow associated with a new business start-up. Finally they rented the Anchorage house to the principal of Lake Otis Elementary.

To reach the newly remodeled office, one entered through the home's back door, passed by the steps and door to the private residence, and proceeded down the stairway to the basement. A hallway on the left led to a waiting room at the other end of the basement. The receptionist (for the time being, Myrt) was seated at a desk near a large rock fireplace in the waiting room. File cabinets were arranged nearby. The waiting room contained an impressive aquarium. A laboratory housed the x-ray machine and centrifuge, a machine for conducting blood analysis. A small x-ray developing room was situated off the main hallway. The office area included a patient restroom and two examination rooms. The doctor's personal office could also be used as an exam room. Employing the skills she acquired while working as a bookkeeper in Houston, Myrt set up the accounting ledgers that would be used over the course of the practice. They were almost ready to get started.

With a Little Help from their Friends

New to the community, without money, and trying to start a business, the Humes were in need of some help—the unsolicited kind. They got just what they needed. Alvin DeJulio, owner and publisher of the newspaper, extended them credit for ad space. They didn't need to pay him until the practice was firmly established. Similarly, Neal Wright supplied them drugs that were common stock for a physician's office, on a credit basis. No hurry for payment there either. Something else was going on, too. A positive buzz had been generated—the townspeople were talking about the new doctor in town. He was a young one too, fresh from practicing in the States, and no doubt "up" on the latest medical procedures and advancements. Excitement about the new doctor was felt at Valley Presbyterian Hospital as well, for a number of reasons. The financially-strapped institution looked forward to the income that would be generated by an active staff surgeon. Instead of sending patients to Anchorage, more could be operated on in Palmer. When Dr. Hume applied for staff membership at the hospital, it was more than happily granted. On September 1, 1958, Dr. Hume's home office opened to the public. That first day, Dr. Hume saw six patients. He and Myrt agreed they were off to a good start; they were going to be okay.

A Narrow Escape

About two months after they opened the practice, the Hume's fifth child was born, a daughter named Starr. Everything seemed new—a new town, a new business, a young family, and now a new addition. The future looked bright, but it was almost over before it started.

Just after Christmas, a children's skating party was held on Wasilla Lake near Williwaw Lodge. The entire Hume family attended. Besides skating, the children were treated to small red fishnet stockings filled with popcorn balls, fruit, and peanuts. Everyone had a good time. With darkness approaching, Dr. Hume pulled his Jeep station wagon around on the ice and the family piled inside. The kids set about removing their skates as the Jeep took off across the lake, taking a well-used winter shortcut to reach the road back to Palmer. As he was driving, the doctor saw some moose tracks cross the traveled way. On impulse, he veered to follow them. At a narrow channel dividing two bodies of lake water, the Jeep, without warning, plunged through the ice. The doctor had been unaware of a spring in the vicinity. There the ice was way too thin to support the weight of a vehicle. When the Jeep broke through the ice and entered the water, enough ice wedged below the undercarriage to provide some buoyancy and a little time for escape. Not knowing how much time they had—already the icy water was high up on the car doors—the doctor, steady as can be, began directing their escape. Suspecting the nearby ice shelf was incapable of supporting any of their body weights, he quickly surmised that baby Starr stood the best chance for survival because she alone could be thrown onto the safety of thicker ice. It was a gamble, throwing the seven-week-old child across the ice, but their options were few and growing fewer as the seconds ticked away. Starr, warmly bundled, was passed through the window and tossed clear of the open water. Next, the other children were quickly ushered through the windows onto the remaining ice shelf. Incredibly, the ice held. The doctor was the last one out of the Jeep and, as his foot cleared the window, the car slipped below the surface of the lake.

Myrt went to her baby. Starr wasn't moving or making a sound, and Myrt feared the worst. Myrt removed her baby's sock and pinched her foot, which elicited a cry. Starr was alive. Then the gravity of the situation began to sink in. The actual event had happened so fast, and the doctor had responded with such calm, that the fear of death had not overwhelmed them. But now, with the lights of the Jeep still glowing beneath seven feet of deadly frigid water, it was all so very real. In the darkness, the family backed away from the accident scene and turned toward the lights of the lodge.

Back to Business

Averting a near tragedy on Wasilla Lake intensified the bond among the family members, but the Humes had an active school, work, and social schedule, and the near death episode was soon put behind them. During the week, Myrt got the older children up and off to school. The doctor rose to his regular breakfast concoction of raw eggs, tomato juice, and Tabasco sauce. Then he made his morning hospital rounds, returning home by 9:00 A.M. to open the basement office. He would work in his private practice until 5:00 P.M. when he closed the office and returned to the hospital to make evening rounds.

His office was closed on Wednesdays, Saturday afternoons, and all day Sunday. The hospital emergency room, however, was never closed. When Dr. Hume first arrived in Palmer, the hospital had no rotating emergency room schedule for doctors. Doctors were called upon to treat their own private practice patients when emergency situations arose at the hospital. The doctor was therefore always on call. Additionally, their local landmark of a house may have been a blessing aesthetically, but it was a curse for the doctor professionally. Everyone knew where the doctor lived, and he lived where he worked. It was easy and convenient for patients to stop by the Hume house, even after hours, to receive care.

First Impressions

The Humes had been in town long enough for the locals to form some very favorable and lasting personal impressions of the family. The kids were well-mannered, respectful, bright, and beautiful. The doctor's wife was tall, slender, and elegant. Myrt was a woman of taste and beauty who seemed to always have on the right clothes. She deflected compliments with a wave of her hand, stating that she was nothing more than a "poor Texas girl." Myrt was bubbly and outgoing. Sometimes she seemed a little blunt and outspoken, but her appearance may have contributed to those notions as tall, beautiful women can be imposing before they even utter a sentence. Initially, it seemed Myrt and the doctor were a rather mismatched couple in terms of appearance and general demeanor, but soon it became obvious that the opposite was true. The more people were around the couple, the more they realized that the two were a great team. Their differences seemed to complement the relationship. In time, most people realized that the doctor had married, quite possibly, the only woman who could handle him.

With a nice house, bright children, a beautiful wife, and an important profession of high social standing, Dr. Hume had it all. As if that wasn't enough, he was a regular sort of guy, entirely without pretense. Although still new to the community, it was as if Dr. Hume had been there all along. In a short time, he was already a true local. He even *looked* liked them—no fancy suits and ties for Dr. Hume. Sure, when he worked, he looked professional in a white shirt and slacks, but even then he wore his collar open. Out among the people, he was often seen in jeans and wool work shirts. And there were plenty of opportunities to see him, particularly for those who frequented the local bars.

After his evening hospital rounds, Dr. Hume rarely returned home for dinner with his family. Instead, he visited a number of the town's drinking establishments. On many occasions he would enter with a flourish, ordering drinks for the house. Then he would settle into fellowship in this nearly all male environment with his fellow patrons. He wasn't one for small talk; conversational trivialities annoyed him. But he was open to talk of just about anything of content, from the high-minded to the decidedly less so. He was unlike anyone most of the townspeople had ever met. He was an intellectual with street smarts—a product of his seemingly incompatible education and his upbringing.

A casual Dr. Hume, downtown with Myrt. (*Hume family collection*)

He was smart, but he didn't have to boast about it. He had a bit of an edge to him, but he didn't play the tough guy. On the town he was accessible to everyone, no matter their social position. People liked that, and respected him for it. He palled around with them. Often, after a night of revelry, the bar crowd went to the Frontier Restaurant for breakfast, and the doctor went too. He ordered his "cannibal sandwich" consisting of raw hamburger topped with raw eggs. He was a fun guy to hang out with. Perhaps most of all, the people of Palmer liked the fact that the doctor liked them.

Though he mixed with everyone, Dr. Hume had a group of closer friends with whom he shared much in common, including Julius Moor, Al Ose, Jim Pazaruski, and Mason LaZelle—all young, highly-intelligent professional men. Neal Wright, older than the others, was perhaps his closest friend. Dr. Hume and Neal shared a similar educational background, both were rich in street smarts, and they both liked to have a drink. Neal loved to play pool and so did the doctor. They spent hours in the basement of Neal's home, shooting pool, drinking, and talking. A lot of their talk was of money, as both men understood and played the stock market, and both had a knack for picking winning stocks. Each of them also made a number of shrewd real estate investments. Neal Wright had many similarities to the doctor's father, John Hume, with his sometimes rascally ways, intelligence, and amazing generosity. Surely this could not have been lost on Dr. Hume.

An Emerging Legend

In Palmer, Dr. Hume was a standout in his field from the very beginning. Shortly after he arrived, a female patient at the hospital went into cardiac arrest, and Dr. Hume performed manual massage directly to the heart in an attempt to maintain circulation during the arrest. It was an audacious move. Would any of the other local doctors have attempted such a procedure? It worked, and the news spread quickly in the small town.

Most people had absolute confidence in him, even faith. A large measure of that confidence was, no doubt, a reflection of the hospital staff's high regard for Dr. Hume. If a person arrived at the hospital in dire need of care, the nurses prayed the patient would ask for Dr. Hume. He was the nurses' overwhelming choice if the chips were down. They had seen him in action. He was unflappable in the emergency room. He prepared for surgery by reviewing a book of surgical protocols, and they knew when he mumbled during surgery, he was reciting, verbatim, the material he had read. The nurses had witnessed his speed and efficiency in the operating room. They also had witnessed the favorable results of his surgeries. They wondered among themselves and to others how Palmer had been so lucky to have received such a gifted physician. They figured this doctor was skilled enough to have written his own ticket to a truly important medical position anywhere.

The nurses also knew that he wasn't always easy to work with, for as his legend grew, so did the demands on his time. It didn't take long for clients to shift from the other doctors in town to Dr. Hume. As the community's expectations of him rose, so did his expectations of himself, as well as his expectations of other medical professionals. He expected the staff at the hospital to be prepared. Always. For everything. He talked about each procedure as he was working, and then expected the staff to be prepared in the future, based on the lessons of the day. Childbirth, his favorite part of the practice, was an area in which he particularly required preparedness and competency. He wanted to be accurately briefed by phone of the progress of the labor. He wanted to arrive when needed, and not before. Certainly he didn't want to be late, but getting to the hospital hours early was a waste of his valuable time. When he did arrive, he wanted to be ready to work; he wanted preparations to have been made. Like so many highly intelligent or gifted people, he was frustrated by those who didn't learn as quickly as he did. On occasion he let his frustrations be known. Because of his high expectations, he soon trusted and relied upon some staff members more than others.

His patients regarded him highly. They could tell he took his work, and thereby his patients' health, extremely seriously. He was a straight talker. His bedside manner was comforting but not coddling, and he sometimes used humor to relieve a patient's fearfulness. Once, a man he knew well reported to the emergency room in fear of losing his sight. The man had been working on his car when he received a shot of hot motor oil to his eyes and face. Upon examination Dr. Hume told him, "There's nothing I can do for your face. You were already ugly anyway, so no matter. I'll just go ahead and save your eyes. That, I can do." The man's eyesight was restored, and he had no facial scarring as a result of the burns.

Certainly Dr. Hume loved a challenge, great or small. One day he noticed that one of the hospital nurses had a ganglion, or cyst, on her wrist. He asked her if she wanted him to take care of it for her. She responded that no, she'd already had several surgeries to remove it, and the ganglion had returned each time. Dr. Hume told her he could remove it for good. The two exchanged good-natured banter on the order of "can not," "can too." Finally they struck a deal; Dr. Hume would attempt to remove the ganglion. If he was successful, then that was that, but if the ganglion reappeared, as it always had before, he would forfeit the full cost of the surgery. He performed the surgery, and the ganglion never returned. When the nurse marveled at his success, he stated with a smile that he had to dig all the way to her toes to get it all.

The respect he earned at the hospital extended to his office practice as well. In short order, he gained the reputation for being a brilliant diagnostician. Much of his success in this area stemmed from his approach. He was absolutely dedicated to taking all the time required to draw out of the patient the information he needed to make an accurate diagnosis. Although extremely busy, he was never in a rush with a patient, and he was renowned for his thoroughness. At least one of his patients, after having moved to Anchorage, made trips back to Palmer to see Dr. Hume for checkups. Another Palmer resident had a routine of traveling to Rochester, Minnesota every few years to visit the Mayo Clinic for a full checkup. One year, the Mayo Clinic doctor performing the examination noticed the patient hailed from Palmer. The doctor asked why the man had gone to all the trouble to travel to Minnesota, when one of the finest doctors around, Dr. Hume, practiced right in Palmer. When the man returned to Palmer, the story did too, and it spread quickly.

His office practice gained a positive reputation in other ways too. He didn't gouge patients with high costs. Dr. Hume's office visit charges, $5 in the beginning but never more than $7.50, were kept below the prevailing Anchorage rate. Even those costs were too high for some. Sensing a hardship, he discreetly asked Myrt not to bill certain patients. Sometimes patients did not have liquid assets, but they did have eggs, milk, or vegetables to trade, and that too was considered adequate payment for medical services. Of course some financially-able patients just wouldn't pay, and while he expected people to pay their bills, he never made any real effort to collect what he was due and never employed a collection agency. As the receptionist and billing clerk, Myrt found non-payers who had the ability to pay to be a frustration. She sometimes called to make friendly debt reminders, but her husband frowned on this and she stopped.

If Dr. Hume had a failing in patient care, it was in maintaining a professional distance between himself and his patients. His display of sincere concern for his patients exceeded that of most medical professionals. The negative impact of this lack of distance was felt by him alone. His sensitivity for the suffering of people—especially children, was acute, and it haunted him. His obvious expressions of compassion only increased his patients' endearment for him. They didn't want to disappoint or frustrate him. If a patient had discontinued taking prescribed medicine and had suffered a relapse, the patient would likely apologize profusely for not following the doctor's instructions and for wasting his time. Dr. Hume's stock answer in such situations was, "Don't get in the way of healing," meaning that prescribed drugs should be taken for their full intended term and not discontinued as soon as the patient began to feel better. His patients rarely made this mistake twice. Knowing his level of compassion, they freely sought and accepted his advice in a myriad of concerns, from potty training, where he strongly urged a non-aggressive approach, to counseling in sexually-related matters. When female patients had questions they couldn't quite find a way to ask due to embarrassment, he would tactfully suggest the patients discuss the issues with his nurse first as an icebreaker, then they would all meet again so the patients could gain answers to their questions. Over time, many patients learned that seeing a doctor did not have to be an uncomfortable experience.

In short order, the new doctor had become very important to nearly everyone in the community.

An Element of Chaos

Society often has subtle means of correcting inappropriate behavior. Sometimes a friend or colleague will confront an individual regarding his behavior. Sometimes relationships cool off in a faint, but perceptible, ostracizing of the erring person. Generally, the intervention is done by someone the individual accepts as a superior or at least a peer. But it's hard to find a person who is a superior or even a peer to the man who has it made. Men who are perceived to have it made are hard to rein in; they are often allowed to do as they wish. So it was that Dr. Hume's increasingly shocking behavior went virtually unchecked.

As Dr. Hume's workload and pressures increased, so did his partying. The night-after-night treks to the bars after his final hospital rounds began to have a noticeable effect on his behavior. Of course his overindulgence resulted in intoxication, but of equal importance, his late-night escapades also left him with woefully inadequate rest. Sleep deprivation and the overuse of alcohol caused him to be moody and unpredictable.

His inhibitions loosened too. Never one to suffer fools gladly, Dr. Hume now commented on remarks made by others that he found particularly inane. Having a great wit and an acid tongue, his verbal barbs could be felt long after they were uttered. His lack of inhibitions extended to his professional life too. He left bar telephone numbers as contacts for the hospital emergency room. When called upon to serve, he regularly attempted take the edge off his drunkenness by breathing from the hospital's medical oxygen cylinders before attending to patients.

The family's home life was affected as well. Too much work, not enough sleep, and too much drink made for an atmosphere of uncertainty and even dread. When will he be home? What will his mood be when he gets here?

Day after Day

Ordinarily, a man's duty as a husband and father is his top priority. But for someone with legendary status, based on his repeated lifesaving "miracles," the community came first. This meant that Dr. Hume always fell short of expectations at home. Unable to separate himself from his occupation, he gave at the office, and there wasn't much left for him to give at home. That doesn't mean he didn't love his wife and children. He did. But the perceived enormity of his family's expectations on him made his home feel less like a sanctuary. A young family's house is abuzz with activities, chatter, and interaction. The children wanted to talk to their father and, being children, were not always articulate or concise. The doctor wanted the abbreviated version of everything. He didn't really want to talk at all while he was home—he did plenty of talking in his daily work life—so he rarely initiated conversations at home. His real sanctuary was in solitude, time with his own thoughts, and in reading.

A voracious reader, Dr. Hume enjoyed the poetry of Robert Service, read weekly news magazines, and studied medical journals. He consumed the works of contemporary literary giants like Norman Mailer, Bernard Malamud, and John Updike. One of his favorite Updike novels was *Rabbit, Run,* a book whose central character, Harry Angstrom, attempted to the break out of the constraints of his world. Life seemed empty for Harry Angstrom, and he felt sure something was missing. Dr. Hume must have felt a connection with Angstrom. An infrequent and somewhat uncomfortable visitor to his own home, he felt like an interloper there, especially because it appeared everything was working out fine without him. And it *was* working. Myrt was the typically efficient doctor's wife, running the household and raising the children largely on her own. Myrt understood the importance of love and discipline, and the results of her labors were obvious. Dr. Hume, for whom competence was paramount, trusted his wife implicitly in her domestic efforts.

To better support Myrt in her household duties, personnel changes were made in the basement office where Myrt was still working as the receptionist. First, the Humes hired Liz Thornlow to help with housekeeping and to make lunches. It proved to be a great working relationship and a personal one too. Liz soon felt like one of the family. But Liz was handling the duties that Myrt, who only wanted to be a wife and mother, yearned to do. So Myrt left her job downstairs to concentrate full-time on her growing family's needs. To replace Myrt in her office duties, Elayne Williams was hired. Elayne made a splendid addition to the staff, which now also included full-time office nurse Jessie DeVries and part-time nurse Lyla France.

The private medical practice continued to grow and with it grew demands on the doctor's time. Everyone wanted him for something—professionally, personally, or as a volunteer. He gave dozens of school sports physicals and conducted first aid classes for the region's volunteer fire departments. He traveled regularly to Talkeetna, a small remote town without roads connecting it to the highway system. Initially, he traveled via the Alaska Railroad, then later with his own private plane. The doctor had learned to fly and purchased a Cessna 150 for his medical practice.

He also worked in rotation with Dr. Bailey as the local Public Health Inspector, where his duties included checking the cleanliness of the area's food serving establishments. He volunteered for some pet projects relating to his profession, too. One of those projects was a benefit for the acquisition of a cardioscope. A fundraiser for this purpose was held at the Tropical Gardens bar at which Dr. Hume operated the till.

Although his schedule was hectic to say the least, Dr. Hume did try to find time for recreation. When time permitted, he and

Myrt bowled on a city league team. On one occasion, he was chatting with another bowler behind the players' area when his turn came around. When he finally realized that his team members were clamoring to get his attention and that he was holding up the game, he placed one hand on the back of a chair and vaulted over the row of seats to get back in the game. In doing so, he caught his foot and was sent sprawling, face first. It was a terrible belly flop on the hard floor and everyone fell silent, certain he had been badly injured. Finally, without so much as a movement, and as they all leaned forward, he was heard to utter, "Does anyone know a good doctor?" He rolled over unhurt and laughed in embarrassment. Much of the fun-loving Vinnie had disappeared but, on occasion, he would still surface. When one of the local fraternal organizations put together a bowling team for an out-of-town tournament, the doctor signed up. It was a three-day trip, and everyone had a terrific time—no one more so than Dr. Hume. His fellow bowlers described him as "a hoot." Still, there were periods when he slipped away from all the revelry to the quiet of his hotel room to relax and read. When the tournament ended and they were preparing to leave for the airport, the men agreed that the only way the trip could be better was if the plane ride back to Palmer was a "champagne flight, just like the rich people take." No one made anything of the joking, idle talk. Assembled at the airport, they were short one man. Dr. Hume was late, and it looked as if he might miss the flight. At the last minute, he ran to catch up with the guys as they boarded the plane. He was moving quickly, carrying a large box that was making the distinctive tinkling sound of bottles bumping. He had bought them all champagne for the flight home. There was one last hurdle however; the flight crew disapproved. The doctor eloquently told the crew about the glorious weekend of fellowship the men had enjoyed and explained that a toast to the outing on the plane ride back was the only fitting finale. And, he went on to say, as their loyal flight crew, they too were entitled to join in the celebration, after the flight of course, whereupon he would present each member of the crew with a complimentary bottle. That did the trick, and the "champagne flight" to Palmer took off.

For Dr. Hume, getting out of town provided the best chance

for relaxation. He took periodic trips to visit his father John in British Columbia. While he was on one of those trips, Myrt, who hadn't gone along, experienced a medical emergency. She was pregnant again and was having some difficulties. She visited a doctor in Anchorage who informed her that the baby had probably died. While awaiting test results to confirm this, Myrt returned to Palmer. Before those results could be relayed, she miscarried. Days later, she began to hemorrhage—badly. With no time to travel to Anchorage, she went to the Palmer hospital, where a local doctor examined her and she was admitted. The doctor told Myrt to get settled, and that he would attend church services and then return to the hospital and check her progress. The situation became dire very quickly. Lyla France, working her hospital shift, understood the gravity of Myrt's changing condition and made an urgent call to the church requesting the attending doctor's immediate return. He got back to the hospital with little time to spare, as Myrt had lost a lot of blood. After this near-death experience, Myrt recalled watching from above as the healthcare team worked feverishly to keep her alive. All this transpired while Dr. Hume was traveling on the Alaska Highway. When he phoned the house to check in, he was surprised to hear Jessie DeVries's voice. She explained she was staying with the children because of Myrt's hospitalization. Despite being told his wife was going to be okay, he became sick with worry and traveled nearly nonstop at high speeds to return to her. It was a troubling end to an otherwise pleasant vacation, but he was tremendously relieved to find his wife safe and on the mend.

The doctor also took a number of trips as part of his continuing education. Though these were work-related excursions, they were often situated in locales suited for relaxation. One such working vacation took him to Mexico City for a seminar conducted by the UCLA Medical School, followed by the annual College of Surgeons Conference in the same city. While in Mexico, he found time to take in saltwater fishing. On a Mexican fishing charter, Dr. Hume landed a great sailfish which he had mounted and hung in his basement office. The sailfish became the focal point of the office waiting room.

With business flourishing and with financial gains from some wise stock market picks, the Humes broadened their investments locally. They purchased real estate and later bought into the construction of several motel buildings to be built a short distance north of their home. They eventually purchased their business partner's interest in the four-unit Pioneer Motel. Myrt ended up managing the enterprise: showing the rooms, collecting the rent, cleaning, and washing the linen. The rentals were an albatross for Myrt as the business was conducted out of their private living quarters. She found it especially maddening when guests left filthy cabins for her to clean. One winter storm damaged one of the buildings to the point of needing immediate repair for fear of losing the roof. Consequently, there was Myrt, in minus ten degree weather with high winds, assisting Bud Haire as he secured the roof. So much for the lofty status of being a doctor's wife.

Much had changed for the Humes in their first few years in Palmer. They had moved from near poverty to relative financial comfort. Business was prospering. The children were growing up. After arriving as a stranger, Dr. Hume had earned the respect, friendship, and love of the community. But in the midst of all these changes, one aspect of their lives remained constant. Dr. Hume couldn't stay out of the bars.

A few people in the community kept a watch on Dr. Hume's activities, and they made some noise about what they didn't like. This vocal minority told friends, neighbors, and each other about the "despicable behavior" they witnessed or heard about. Enough of this talk reached the hospital board that one of the young directors screwed up his courage and paid the doctor a visit. He suggested to the doctor that perhaps he was drinking too much. Dr. Hume explained that a doctor's life is full of pressure and that doctors have to have some sort of relief. The director then suggested that maybe Dr. Hume could limit his drinking to his off-duty time. In response, Dr. Hume reminded him that there was never a time when he was off duty.

Dr Hume's drinking continued unabated and so did the stories about his drinking. One night, a new teacher in town was escorted by a co-worker on a tour of the local watering holes. Upon entering the Palmer Bar, the new guy was challenged to guess the occupation of an obviously intoxicated man seated at the bar. The inebriate was attired in working man's clothes; he sat slumped with his head hung low. His hair was in his eyes. The new resident was stumped. "Let me tell you," his co-worker replied. "You're looking at the town doctor."

Eric

The Hollembaek family was visiting friends when sons Scott and Eric went outside to play hide-and-seek. Scott found a hiding spot and waited for his little brother to find him, but the three-year-old never came. Scott, who was six years older, poked his head out to ascertain his brother's whereabouts. Scott didn't see him. Leaving his hiding spot, he went looking for Eric, but still couldn't find him. Scott's attention was drawn to a commotion over at the nearby sled dog lot. It appeared that a large chained husky was vigorously shaking a doll. In an instant the horrible realization hit Scott that it was no doll. It was Eric. Eric had wandered in among the dogs. Without caution, Scott ran to save his little brother. Yelling and screaming and throwing anything he could find, Scott advanced on the big dog. The husky retreated and cowered to the confines of his doghouse giving up the torn little boy without a fight. Scott pulled Eric's limp, nearly lifeless body away from his attacker. The boy's injuries were so severe that even the most optimistic family member couldn't image he would survive. Eric was gathered up and the Hollembaeks drove as fast as they could for the hospital in Palmer. Dr. Hume took the phone call from the emergency room and then he too headed for the hospital as fast as he could.

The doctor stepped into near bedlam: a horribly mauled little boy, parents justifiably overwrought and in agony with concern, and a nursing staff at their professional limits trying to maintain control over the situation and the patient. Dr. Hume slipped smoothly into his role as the captain of the medical team and was calm and clearheaded. Off to surgery they went. A physical examination revealed the seriousness of Eric's injuries. He had deep, jagged lacerations to the back of his neck and to his throat, extending into his abdomen. Extensive nerve damage to the neck was highly probable. The wounds contained dog saliva and the filthy feces-ridden dirt of the dog lot. Eric had lost a tremendous amount of blood. So much trauma to such a little boy. The team went to work, with Dr. Hume in complete control. His calm transferred, as if by osmosis, to the others.

The doctor instructed a nurse to shave Eric's head, but when she attempted to do so she found his scalp wouldn't stay put. The scalp had been torn away from his head during the attack. Flustered, the nurse confessed that she could not perform the task. Calmly, Dr. Hume told her it had to be done and she was the one who had to do it. He took the electric shears from her and patiently showed her how the task was to be performed and how the clippings were to be kept free from the wound. Then, placing the shears in her hands once more, and without another look, he turned to resume his work.

Meanwhile, outside the operating room, Eric's father was overcome with emotion, yelling out for the staff, and for God, to save his boy. In anguish and frustration he pounded his fists on the walls. This could all be heard inside the operating room and it was unsettling, but the doctor was unfazed, deep in concentration, and that helped steady everyone. In the midst of the hours-long operation, the boy's heart stopped. The doctor restarted it. Later, it stopped again and Dr. Hume started it again. As the team worked on, cleaning and closing the wounds, Eric's heart stopped several more times, only to be restarted. At last they finished. The final tally from the dog attack was grim: the loss of a lung and a kidney, nerve damage, and 300 stitches to put him back together. After doing all they could, they waited. The nurses watched over the little boy with extra care. Dr. Hume visited him during his usual morning and evening rounds, but he turned up to see Eric at other times too. He would quietly come in and check on the boy and leave just as quietly. A week passed before Eric made even the slightest perceptible improvement, but he made steady minor progress from then on. Finally, it became apparent that although more hospitalization and extensive rehabilitation would be necessary, Eric would survive the ordeal. The Hollembaeks would forever believe Dr. Hume was nothing short of a miracle worker. Those who saw him in action during these pivotal hours in the life of that little boy agreed.

Once Eric had passed out of harm's way, the community seemed to exhale as one, so relieved that he was going to make it. Dr. Hume left town. Once he knew the boy was going to be all right, he made an escape. It was nothing but a day trip, but he needed to leave town, even if just for a short time.

He flew down to Kalgin Island near Kenai, a summer commercial fishing camp for several Palmer families, landing on the beach between tides. He wasn't there to sport fish, but to ease his troubled mind. While there, he sought out a friend and related the case of the mauled child. Distraught, he lamented that he had not done enough for the boy, that he should have been able to help him more. He said he felt inadequate and useless. He stayed a little longer, then he had to leave and return to Palmer before the tide stranded him there.

A Tough Crowd

As much as Dr. Hume loved people, certain aspects of human nature confounded him. He didn't understand the judgmental side of people, especially when it concerned the poor treatment or labeling of young individuals. When two local teenage girls became pregnant, they were shunned and treated with disdain. The doctor reacted to the situation with respect and understanding for the girls. He understood the consequences of teenage pregnancy, but once a pregnancy had occurred he didn't see the use in persecuting those involved. His understanding of human sexuality ran counter to the social stigmas that were often used as an attempt at birth control. Not wanting one of his own children to befall the harsh treatment that society was quick to mete out, he spoke with his daughter April about sex, birth control, and responsibility. For her part, April felt truly informed on the subject and knew she was responsible for making good decisions.

Road Trip

In the spring of 1962, the Valley Theatre Guild presented a production of *Lo and Behold,* a comedy showcasing the talents of local thespians Larry Kincaid, Jack Riley, Harry Evans, Muriel Wattum, and Gary Brown. Also starring in the play, cast as ghosts, were Kitty Johnson, Jack Dodge, and Myrt Hume. The shows, performed at the Central School gym, were well-attended and received. Where once he would have played a strong part in such a production, now the doctor did not even attend a single performance of a show in which his wife was featured.

While Myrt was practicing for her part in the play, she and the children were also making plans for a fantastic summer vacation. They decided to undertake a long car trip from Alaska to Texas and back again, with lots of fun stops in between. They arranged to leave just after school let out and prepared to be gone for the summer.

June

When his family had been gone for less than a month, events conspired to undo Dr. Hume's summer. A young Anchorage woman drove to Palmer on a Friday afternoon, checked into the Matanuska Hotel, and took her life. On Saturday, hotel employees found her and called Police Chief Louis Bencardino, who notified Magistrate Dorothy Saxton and Dr. Hume. Dr. Hume's initial examination of the body and the scene confirmed that the death was likely a suicide. For Dr. Hume, the investigation was one of real sadness. Though he hadn't known the woman, the loss of her life had an effect on him. As a person who had dedicated his life to helping preserve the lives of others, suicide seemed an appalling disregard for the essence of his profession. On an emotional level, he couldn't help but wonder what in her life had defeated her so that she could not find the hope to live one more day.

The weekend was just getting started. On the following evening, Thurman and Francis Betts returned along with another couple to their Wasilla Lake home after attending the annual summer picnic for one of the local fraternal organizations. It was a chilly evening and they decided to build a fire. In an effort to quickly start the blaze, fuel oil was poured on the fireplace logs. Someone noted that the amount of accelerant used seemed excessive, so they decided to wait for awhile before striking a match, allowing some of the fuel to evaporate. What they did not know was that the fuel ran to the bottom of the fireplace and over the hearth, passing out into the room where the two couples were seated in close proximity to the fireplace. After some time had passed, they judged it was safe enough to start the fire. When the match was put to the logs, a flash of flames erupted, and a line of fire bolted across the floor, following the path of the fuel. The streak of fire ran to where the fuel had pooled under a plastic chair that held Francis Betts. The chair was almost instantly engulfed in flames and it quickly melted around her body. The other couple immediately transported Francis to the hospital in Palmer. Thurman successfully battled the home fire then followed. At the hospital, Dr. Hume examined the burned woman and began attempts at saving her. Given the nature and extent of her injuries, visitors were not allowed to see her, but the doctor could not bear to allow her to suffer alone. He stayed at her bedside, attending to her and holding her hand. She rallied briefly, giving hope that she would be able to withstand a flight to a Lower 48 burn center, but it was not to be. She died only days after the fire. This was a particularly difficult case for Dr. Hume because he knew and liked both Bettses, especially Francis. He grieved her loss and was saddened by the suffering he saw in Thurman. Hume's distress over the accident seemed so deep that he appeared to be diminished by it. Close friends could tell it changed him. Some wondered, despite his profound professional gifts, if he was really cut out be a doctor. It didn't seem a doctor should get that upset about losing a patient.

In the early morning hours on the day funeral services were to be conducted for Francis Betts, Dr. Hume showed up at the hospital drunk and looking for trouble. As he made his way around the hospital, he saw a young, unmarried nurse working in a small room. He entered the room and positioned himself between the nurse and the door. He announced his roguish intentions. He moved forward, reaching for her. She slipped away from him and, feeling unnerved, called her supervisor and reported the incident. Dr. Hume boiled over with anger. He didn't seem perturbed by the spurned advances, but being informed on made him mad. After all, that was not how these things were to be handled; you don't tell on a doctor! But now, with a third party involved, he knew his actions would bring repercussions. In retaliation, he began a nasty verbal assault on the young nurse. Hearing enough of his tirade, Frances Schupp, a nurse's aide, intervened. Standing toe-to-toe, the two argued, neither backing down. Then, the already bad situation got much worse. Dr. Hume lost his temper and got pushy with Mrs. Schupp. She stood her ground. The confrontation continued to escalate. Then, unimaginably, he physically assaulted her, striking her in the face, stomach, and about her arms.

Consequences

The frontier community could overlook a lot of bad behavior, both personally and professionally, but this episode demanded attention. The hospital board was forced to investigate the matter and to take administrative action. Based on their findings, they suspended Dr. Hume's hospital privileges. The board president issued the doctor a letter of suspension. Several board members felt the hospital at least owed him the courtesy of an in-person notification, so two members stopped by his home and delivered the hard news. Upon learning of the suspension, Dr. Hume cursed at them, and slammed the door. The board believed that was the end of it. They made no public decree or disclosure of any kind. It was a private matter carried out confidentially, just the way the profession liked to conduct business. Of course, it wasn't that simple. Although the hospital issued no official announcement of the suspension, the doctor was conspicuously absent from the facility, eliciting unwanted questions. The questions were avoided when Dr. Hume decided to take a six-week "vacation," turning his office practice over to Dr. J. Ronald Brown in the interim.

The Hits Keep Coming

With the doctor out of town, some of the rancor he had created at the hospital began to subside. Despite all the trouble he had caused, the medical professionals missed his abilities. Though he had issued no apologies for his conduct, the fact that he left town could be viewed, if one were particularly charitable, as an act of contrition. To add to this was a small but influential group of citizens, who were in the know regarding recent events and who pushed for the lifting of the suspension. The board acquiesced, hoping Dr. Hume had learned his lesson. Frances Schupp hoped so too, but she didn't see how the doctor would possibly learn anything about professional accountability from such a minor personnel action. She felt alone in her pursuit for some semblance of justice, and decided the only recourse left was through the courts. She sued Dr. Hume for assault in civil court.

About this same time, Dr. Hume received notification that his own mother was suing him too. Gracie had retained legal counsel in the matter of unpaid financial support she claimed was due her from her son, the doctor. The suit had all the markings of a Grover scheme. As ridiculous as the suit was, it was an unpleasantness the doctor was forced to address. He too sought counsel in the matter.

Reunited

Meanwhile, Myrt and the children had the summer vacation of a lifetime. They felt like they had been everywhere and seen everything on their 12,000 mile excursion: Disneyland, Knott's Berry Farm, and all the tourist attractions they could find, topped off, on the return trip, with a visit to the World's Fair in Seattle. From there, they stopped off for a visit with John Hume in British Columbia, where they were joined by Dr. Hume for the Alaska Highway portion of the trip. With everybody back together again, the journey home was great fun too.

Back in Palmer, the doctor finally gave his wife a censored account of his summer activities. He confessed to the pass he made at the nurse and the ensuing scuffle with Frances Schupp. He told Myrt of the Schupp lawsuit and the suit brought by his mother. He left out the part about the suspension and his extended vacation. On the bright side, he reported, he had purchased recreational property on Finger Lake that contained a fixer-upper residence.

The totality of the news was quite a blow for Myrt, but ultimately her husband's problems were hers too, and they took up the fight together. The suit with Mrs. Schupp ended in an out-of-court financial settlement. The matter with Gracie was more heart wrenching. Dr. Hume's attorney advised him to chronicle on paper all of Gracie's shortcomings as a mother. He was directed to write of her abandonment of him and his siblings, how she had taken up with a man of ill character, and all the rest. Dr. Hume agreed to undertake the distasteful task, and wrote down all his bitter memories. After he had finished, he couldn't even bring himself to give the pages to his attorney. He didn't have the stomach for it. He dropped his defense to the trumped-up charges, and paid his mother the forty dollars a month she demanded. This amount was less than he already sent her for birthdays and other occasions throughout the year, but after this gross display of greed, those cash gifts disappeared. Angry letters from Grover regarding money were intercepted by Myrt and destroyed in an attempt to shield her husband from further ugliness.

For the participants in the difficult events of the summer of 1962, the pain lessened with time, but never left entirely. The nurse Dr. Hume made the pass at avoided him, and never felt at ease in his presence again. Mrs. Schupp's level of comfort in the hospital workplace was severely diminished, and she felt a general lack of support from her co-workers and the hospital administration regarding her handling of the assault. Myrt was frustrated by her husband's behavior and that frustration was sometimes quite apparent, but like all married people she was in the business of forgiveness. The hospital board, confronted with an endless stream of challenges in running the hospital, was not as forgiving.

10

The Hospital

To the Rescue

When Dr. Earl Albrecht and the nurses arrived in the Matanuska colony in 1935, they found little in the way of facilities for patient care. A building measuring approximately twenty by thirty feet had been hastily enclosed for use as the valley's first hospital. A tent near the hospital served as Dr. Albrecht's living quarters, a portion of which was partitioned off as an office. The hospital had no utilities. The building had no heat until the addition of a small "lean-to" that housed a wood-fueled cookstove. Dr. Albrecht and Max Sherrod, a colonist and registered nurse, cut and split wood for the stove. Water for the hospital was hauled to a pair of fifty-five gallon drums stationed on an outside platform. The barrels were piped to a sink near the stove, the water fed by gravity. There was no electricity available; the only light came from a few windows and gasoline lamps. Sewer and medical waste disposal services were also unavailable. For this purpose, a pit was dug and a log top was constructed with a disposal opening fitted over the pit.

These were modest facilities, to be sure, but hope was in sight, as construction had begun on a real hospital. The medical personnel endured the primitive conditions that first summer and fall. In the early winter, the staff felt rewarded when the new Valley Hospital, as it was called, was ready for occupancy. The hospital was similar in appearance to the other lapsided buildings in the community. The single story I-shaped building featuring a large number of multi-paned windows. Several steps led to the wood frame double doors of the main entrance, which also featured the multi-pane window design.

The building's interior boasted a lobby area, both men's and women's wards, and twenty beds. The hospital included doctors' offices, a dentist's office, an operating room, a laboratory, and an x-ray room, as well as an examination room and an obstetrical ward. A kitchen, dining room, and boiler room were also in the new building. Electric power was provided by the colony power house, and soon the hospital was connected to the sewer system. The hospital staff included six nurses, a cook and a kitchen assistant, a clerk/receptionist, a full-time doctor, a part-time dentist, and a maintenance man. It was a fine facility with a competent staff. The community was justified in taking pride in its new hospital. The days ahead were not easy and money was always tight, but they persevered. For the next eleven years, the hospital provided quality service to the residents of the valley. Then on May 27, 1946, the fire signals sounded at the Co-op. The volunteer fire department and other local residents responded to a fire at the hospital. Luckily all the patients were evacuated without injury, and most of the hospital's equipment was saved, but the building was a total loss. The structure was not insured.

A Struggle Renewed

In the immediate aftermath of the fire, patients were either sent home or housed in private volunteer homes in or near Palmer. Their treatment continued in a domestic environment through house calls. The school board allowed the hospital to use Central School's classrooms when summer vacation began. Other governmental agencies, businesses, and private citizens stepped up with donations of office space, services, and money, all of which bought the hospital a little time to start over. The Army offered surplus Quonset huts, which were gladly accepted. These were finished structures requiring only some retrofitting and setup to be ready for occupancy. This somewhat ramshackle affair—three Quonset huts attached to a small frame building—became the temporary Valley Hospital. The short-term solution lasted nearly eight years. During that time, the hospital staff faced a number of challenges, most of which were met with creativity and support from the community. Ongoing fundraising took a myriad of forms. Hospital bonds and prepaid hospital certificates redeemable for hospital services

A portion of the temporary hospital with attached Quonset hut at left. (*Stenberg family collection*)

were sold, and church benefits were held. Volunteer work parties accomplished a great deal of maintenance and new construction projects. Local churches furnished meals for workers on a rotating basis. Some of the challenges posed problems with no clear solution. Six years after the fire, the hospital was losing money. Many residents could not pay for their hospital care and would not be able to in the foreseeable future. The Quonset huts' serviceable life was rapidly approaching an end. They were difficult and costly to heat, and when it rained it poured inside them as well. Even if the buildings had been serviceable, the community had outgrown the temporary facilities. Recognizing the need for a new building, the hospital board of directors began making plans and inquiries.

Valley Presbyterian Hospital

A number of groups and agencies were contacted during the search for financial participants in the construction of a new hospital. The Board of National Missions of the Presbyterian Church agreed to assist the community in fundraising. The board also committed to long-term involvement in the new hospital's operation through a building loan. The hospital's funding campaign coincided with the Women of the Presbyterian Church's celebration of seventy-five years of work in the territory. The group adopted the hospital's campaign for its annual project. Miss Elsie Penfield, secretary of women's projects for the Board of Missions, developed a slogan for the ambitious campaign. Playing off her last name, she created the catchy alliteration "Pennies for Palmer." The drive was taken not only throughout the territory but to all the states, putting the small community on the national map for the first time since the days of colonization. The fundraising effort was a startling success, surpassing even the most optimistic projections. The drive brought in an astonishing $232,536. Meanwhile, community leaders sought other sources of revenue. A grant was obtained from the U.S. government, provided for under the Hospital Survey and Construction Act of 1946. The program, better known as the Hill-Burton Act for the sponsoring Senators Lister Hill and Harold Burton, was designed to provide funds to hospitals that had grown obsolete during the financial constraints of the preceding war years and the Great Depression. Palmer was granted Hill-Burton funds in the amount of $344,000. The hospital further benefited from a territorial appropriation of $107,500, and $15,000 was raised locally. The building fund coffers finally stood just short of $700,000.

Once the plans and specifications were complete, the hospital building project was submitted for bids and a contract was awarded to low bidder C.R. Foss, Inc. of Anchorage.

The construction project started off with a huge groundbreaking ceremony attended by hundreds of local residents. Representatives from the City of Palmer, C.R. Foss, the U.S. Public Health Service, the Presbyterian Church, and the hospital board addressed the attendees. The Palmer High School marching band performed in full regalia. The event culminated with Mrs. Bert Bingle, representing the women's organizations of the Presbyterian Church, climbing aboard a dozer and with the assistance of Leo Lucas, breaking ground for the new hospital. The band concluded the afternoon festivities with *God Bless America*.

Almost one year to the day after signing the construction contract with C.R. Foss, and months ahead of schedule, a dedication ceremony was held for the new hospital. There was a large turnout; more than 500 people came to celebrate. Representatives of the same entities that had given speeches at the groundbreaking spoke again. Miss Elsie Penfield was in attendance and was lauded for her impressive fundraising efforts.

Also present was Dr. Albrecht, now Territorial Commissioner of Health, who had, almost twenty years earlier, journeyed north by rail to provide medical aid to the beleaguered colony. Perhaps the best part of the day was when residents were allowed to tour the new facilities. Although they had seen the published architect's drawings of the structure, nothing compared to walking the halls of the modern steel-framed concrete hospital building they could call their own.

The new Valley Presbyterian Hospital. *(Steve McCutcheon photographer, Anchorage Museum at Rasmuson Center)*

The new hospital's public entrance. (*Ward Wells photographer, Anchorage Museum at Rasmuson Center*)

Valley Presbyterian Hospital was laid out, roughly, in the shape of a cross. A covered walkway extended from the gravel parking lot to the front entrance. Upon entering, a visitor would find two public restrooms immediately inside the doorway. Straight ahead was the hospital waiting room. Nearby was the Public Health Center. The front desk and office were across the hall from the main waiting area. Down the hallway from the front desk was a conference room on the right where a number of board meetings were held. Across the hall from the conference room was the nurses' station. A left turn at the nurses' station would take a visitor up a hallway past the nurses' lounge and dining room on the left. The lounge and dining room were also sometimes home to board meetings. At the end of this hallway was the kitchen. Across from the dining room were stairs which led to a basement laundry, storage room, and furnace area. Another wing housed a lab and x-ray room, an isolation room, a patient "lock down" area, and a string of double occupancy patient rooms. Each patient room shared a restroom with the adjoining room. At the end of this wing was the solarium. The hospital also boasted a modern emergency room, nursery, obstetric rooms, labor room, delivery room, surgical room and a central supply room.

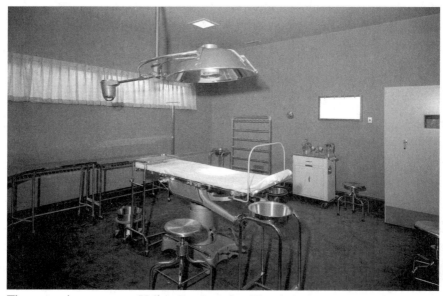

The operating room at Valley Presbyterian Hospital. (*Ward Wells photographer, Anchorage Museum at Rasmuson Center*)

Work still needed to be done such as landscaping, which was undertaken by volunteer forces, and moving furniture and equipment from the old to the new building. Fundraising continued to replace or upgrade existing equipment. But the huge hurdle had been crossed, and now all efforts returned to the challenges of running a hospital.

The Board

The quality of any organization's board of directors is limited by two factors—the number of those in the community who are capable of effective service, and more importantly, from that same group, the number of those willing to serve. The general make-up of the hospital board of directors was no different than any other nonprofit, self-governing entity in Palmer. It included volunteers with a wide range of experience and educational backgrounds. Because the operation of a hospital was such a multifaceted endeavor, directors were called upon during the course of their service to make decisions regarding finances, building maintenance, governmental regulations, and personnel actions, as well as a host of other matters. Many of the issues were big picture concerns, but there were plenty of crisis management matters too. If an issue before the board was outside an individual director's area of expertise, then that director was expected to rely on personal judgment. Each listened to complaints about the staff, the doctors, the building, the food, and about the board's performance. It was all part of community service.

Board members were elected by vote of the general membership at the hospital's mid-February annual meeting. It was an eleven person board with members serving three-year terms. The terms were staggered in intervals with three or more (depending on resignations, if any) board members elected yearly. Following the annual meeting, new and standing board members elected a president, vice president, secretary, and treasurer from within their ranks. Board meetings occurred monthly, unless committee work or a hot issue required more involvement. Most meetings lasted from one to two hours, but many lasted much longer. When getting down to business, most new board members, especially those lacking prior board tenure of any kind, found the experience a revelation. A number of factions were represented within the board, among the employees, and within the general membership. All actively forwarded their own agendas. Certainly most of these agendas were intended to serve the interests of the hospital, but some served others interests as well. This often resulted in conflict which, on occasion, spilled out of the board room and into the press, with reports of general discontent and messy resignations.

One particular issue illustrated the involvement of such factions and their impact on an issue before the board. It played out in the public arena at an annual meeting shortly before the Humes arrived in Palmer. The matter concerned proceeds generated from a raffle. As a fundraiser, the raffle seemed harmless enough. At issue was the group conducting the event. The Liquor Dealers' Association had offered the financially-strapped hospital revenue generated from its raffle. After some debate and a close vote, the board accepted the offer. Next the National Board of Missions weighed in on the matter. The Board of Missions suggested the hospital board rethink its decision. The board did so and decided to put the matter before the general membership for a vote. That's when the fireworks really began, with speakers on both sides of the issue offering impassioned pleas for the Hospital Association to do the "right thing." On one side were those who felt a moral debt was owed to the Presbyterian Church for all it had done to make the hospital possible in the first place. This group also believed the continuing relationship with the church was best served by not accepting the Liquor Dealers' money. On the other side were those who saw the issue in less moralistic terms. The hospital was already losing money and costs were rising. They reasoned that the hospital had a moral obligation to manage its debt properly and pay its creditors. Besides, it was argued, the church did not actually contribute to the yearly operating costs of the hospital; it donated an amount roughly equal to the cost of an insurance premium which the church insisted the Hospital Association carry. The opponents countered, "What if we lose that amount because of this raffle? Aren't we better off with a donation we can depend on year in and year out?" The group speaking for acceptance of the raffle funds offered that if one were to start scrutinizing and casting judgment on the intent of every group or effort made to raise funds for the hospital, little fundraising would ever again be accomplished.

Finally the church weighed in again. The spokesman reiterated that the church was opposed to liquor and gambling, both of which were components of this raffle. The spokesman also stated that this was nothing more than an advisory statement detailing the wishes of the church and that the membership was free to decide the issue. But a letter received later from the

Board of Missions indicated a far stronger stance. This letter sounded a lot like an ultimatum. The debate raged on, finally ending with a close vote of 125 to 120 in support of accepting the funds. The outcome left no real victor. The ramifications were not immediately obvious, but they simmered below the surface in individual, professional, and even institutional hurt feelings, only to erupt again in future issues. Emotional decisions that evenly divide a community, with strong and differing perceptions of right and wrong, are not rare. But only a few are tasked with picking up the pieces of a hotly contested issue and continuing on. Here, it was the hospital's board of directors. In the aftermath of such disputes, the board could almost hear more trouble coming.

It's the Money

Financial concerns continued after the opening of the new hospital. Some patients' inability or unwillingness to pay was a persistent problem. As tends to be the case, several of the highest cost patients fell into that category. At the start of the 1960s, the hospital carried about 110 delinquent accounts. Collection agencies were used at times, but to no great effect. In this area, board members had to exhibit forbearance and diplomacy, for they were keenly aware that a number of impoverished families would not seek needed medical services if they were unable to pay, fearing their delinquent account would be turned over to a collection agency. On occasion, patients paid only part of their bills. Sometimes governmental agencies reimbursed the hospital for up to eighty percent of the actual costs. In an era before assisted living programs, the hospital was also home to several long-term residents suffering from mental illness, alcoholism, or other chronic conditions. Some of these continuing patients were indigent. And sometimes there just weren't enough patients in the hospital to generate the required operating income.

Even the new building itself had problems. The contractor corrected a number of minor issues during the warranty phase, but one significant problem remained. From the beginning, the roof leaked badly. The flaw was at the intersection of the cross design, the largest expanse of the flat roof. During winter freeze-thaw cycles, ten to fifteen buckets had to be utilized inside to catch the flow, creating an area the nurses laughingly referred to as "the obstacle course." A maintenance worker undertook the laborious task of roof snow removal and monitoring and emptying the buckets. The leaks were blamed on a poorly functioning expansion joint, but whatever the cause, the effect was a drain on the hospital's human and financial resources.

Day-to-day expenses were the most unrelenting. The hospital was already years behind in paying its electricity and water bills. In a bold move, the hospital board even suggested that a share of Palmer's sales tax be allocated for payment of the water bill. The Department of Labor earnestly sought the hospital's unpaid contributions to the Unemployment Compensation Fund from the period of early 1954 to the end of 1959, a sum totaling more than $7,000. The hospital was also in arrears to about ten local vendors and almost twice as many outside the area. Eventually, some creditors would only deal with the hospital on a cash basis. Drug salesmen presented a unique problem for the administration, for while the hospital was delinquent in payment to these vendors too, it had a dire need for the free samples these salesmen distributed. The continuing question was always who was to be paid first, and how much?

With community-spirited generosity, a number of businesses wrote off all or a portion of the hospital's debt with the understanding that accounts would be kept current from that point forward. Matanuska Electric Association wrote off the hospital's entire delinquent account. In a few cases, patients who had experienced medical recovery but were unable to pay for their services were offered jobs at the hospital to work off their debt. Some of these former patients, with training, proved to be valuable assets. And the roof was finally repaired. Albeit slowly, ground was gained for the hospital's financial footing, in no small part due to the diligence of all those involved in its operation, and with contributions from the community.

The Volunteer Effort

Community involvement was absolutely essential to the success of the hospital. A multitude of organizations, including the American Legion, Veterans of Foreign Wars, Kiwanis, Boy and Girl Scouts, PTA, and homemakers' clubs, to name a few, sponsored a wide range of projects designed to assist the hospital.

Raffle tickets were sold for movie cameras and other prizes with the proceeds going to the hospital. Benefits such as Christmas bazaars, minstrel shows, and even boxing matches were staged to help.

One organization, the hospital auxiliary, had as its sole purpose the furthering of the goals of the hospital. The hospital auxiliary was a group of women who worked tirelessly in an unending stream of fundraisers. The auxiliary served refreshments at the hospital, and at the electric and telephone association's annual meetings. They sold postcards of the hospital and took Polaroid snapshots of newborns which they sold to the mothers for fifty cents apiece. They held bake sales, which involved almost everyone in the area as a contributor, purchaser, or both. In another effort to raise funds, which seems laughable in present times, the hospital auxiliary operated the cigarette machine at the hospital. Funds raised by the auxiliary purchased an obstetrics table, a blood refrigerator, a steam vaporizer, blood pressure cuffs, and many more large and small items. The auxiliary performed other work too, including sewing projects that supplied the hospital with curtains, nursery pads, surgical towels, and children's pajamas.

In addition to the clubs, organizations, and auxiliary, the hospital received support from many businesses and private citizens, both in monetary donations and in free labor. As is human nature, some donors expected certain benefits or privileges in return for their generosity. No express strings were attached, but perhaps there was an expectation that the input of those giving so much might enjoy more consideration, perhaps a little more weight than others on a given issue. That influence was never intentionally granted, certainly not to the extent desired by those who believed they had earned it.

The Nurses

The hospital nurses truly gave at the office for, in addition to their occupation, they supported the hospital through a variety of altruistic efforts. They helped in the fundraisers sponsored by the various organizations, but they took on other work too. They planted flowers, washed windows, and painted, enhancing the facility's appearance without additional cost. They also worked extra hours unpaid. They were close-knit, with a true spirit of camaraderie. The nurses' work day was usually comprised of three eight-hour shifts. The number of nurses working each shift was determined by the patient count, or census, as it was called. Generally, two nurses and two aides worked the 8 A.M. to 4 P.M. day shift. The 4 P.M. to midnight shift was handled by at least one nurse and a nurse's aide, and the 12 A.M. to 8 A.M. shift was covered by a nurse and an aide. A typical shift included dispensing medications and food, seeing to patient needs, charting, OB and ER work, and assisting the physicians on rounds and in surgery. And then there was sterilizing and cleaning, a constant and ongoing effort that paid dividends in the hospital's low infection rate. Each shift reported pertinent information to the next, and each shift performed a count of the medications on hand.

There were, of course, other duties as assigned. Nurses held the role of enforcer too. Hospitals in the 1960s were quite restrictive in a number of matters such as visiting hours. When those hours were over, nurses would dutifully shoo visitors from the rooms. Other rules were strictly observed too: no visitors under the age of sixteen, a maximum of two visitors per patient per visit, no exceptions. Visitors were not allowed to sit on the patient's bed or use the restroom. The hospital was supposed to be a quiet place, and this included the grounds. Little Leaguers warming up on the hospital lawn in preparation for their evening game (the Palmer Little League field was just across the street) were often told to go elsewhere. Enforcement of the rules went with the nurses' territory, and it was not harsh but it was firm. They were uniformed, full-time, front line registered professionals who felt a strong allegiance to their profession and to the hospital.

11

The Gathering Storm

The Devil's Radio

Gossip is the most harmful weapon used in character assassination. Its practitioners can be either skilled or unskilled and still be highly effective. Gossipers may ply their trade with or without ill intent and still achieve the same result. It is truly a double-edged sword, for while gossip impugns character, it simultaneously obscures the truth. Obscuring the truth with negative—or even larger than life pseudo-positive impressions—is the cornerstone of gossip.

Many stories were told of Dr. Hume's stint in the military, about how he was traumatized as a result of having to treat Korean War wounded without anesthesia. The stories, based on a false pretense of battlefront service, lent a heroic or even patriotic justification to his overindulgence with alcohol.

Stories also circulated endlessly of Dr. Hume receiving emergency room calls while in his cups at local taverns. Upon receiving a call, the doctor, falling down drunk and barely able to find his way out the door, would stagger from the establishment, get in his car, drive to the hospital, take a few deep breaths of medical oxygen, be right as rain, and set about the important business of saving lives. Laughs and guffaws would punctuate these stories with tag lines that added, "He must have emptied an entire oxygen tank trying to get sober that time!"

There were many stories about him working through a bad case of the tremors, claiming that his doctoring abilities were so awesome that he could will the shaking away during a procedure. Stories such as these, while containing elements of truth,

153

gave the impression that Dr. Hume was superhuman, and that the standard rules did not apply to him.

With no limitations as to truth, scale, or proportion, these and many more whispered tales built a legend completely apart from, and often obscuring, his humanity and actual good deeds. Additionally, this kind of legendary status removed most standards of personal responsibility, to be replaced with blind acceptance.

The Toast of the Town

Dr. Hume smarted awhile from his run-in with Mrs. Schupp, the associated lawsuit, and hospital suspension, but most of this business was conducted without public knowledge, so there was a lesser element of embarrassment attached than might have been. It didn't take long for him to resume his night-time activities and be out among the people. The locals still very much enjoyed his company, but there was an increasingly harder edge to the doctor's personality while he was drinking. His always-present sarcastic wit surfaced with more regularity. Sometimes, in a dark mood, he drank alone, listening to the conversations of nearby patrons. He interjected observations on what was being said, particularly if he sensed the conversation was meant to impress him. If someone grandly proclaimed that he had read an important book or article, Dr. Hume might react with a cynical, "I read too." He was annoyed with mispronounced words and would correct, "It's not prostrate, it's *prostate.*" Sometimes his interjections were much harsher.

The most frustrating aspect of Dr. Hume's public life was the continual interruptions by those seeking medical advice. Out for dinner or out for drinks, it didn't matter where or when, somebody always wanted something from him. He could absolutely count on an intrusion of some kind. Sometimes he listened carefully and provided the sought after advice, but on other occasions he reacted poorly to the requests for on the spot diagnosis and lashed out verbally. The intrusions were often countered with his own brand of black humor. On one of the Wednesdays he had off, he was sitting at a bar having a drink with Bob Munford, the town barber, when in walked a man who, after surveying the occupants of the tavern, made a beeline for Dr. Hume. The man unleashed a torrent of complaints on the doctor, ranting and raving about the fact that the doctor's office was closed and that the doctor had been hard to find and most importantly that he was sick, oh so very sick. Standing next to the doctor's barstool, and making something of a spectacle of himself, he recounted each and every ache, pain, and symptom he had endured. Finally, as he was nearly played out with talk, he at last asked, "Doctor, what is wrong with me?" and stood breathlessly waiting for the response. Dr. Hume, who had listened intently throughout the harangue, put his hand on the man's shoulder for emphasis, looked him square in the eye, and after a pregnant pause solemnly said, "You are going to die." The remark was so absurd, unexpected, and well-timed, that even the man had to laugh.

Dr. Hume's drinking extended through the entire chain of local venues. He had his favorites, but no establishment was too high- or lowbrow for Dr. Hume to visit and engage the clientele in conversation or merriment. Despite his sometimes acid tongue, his fellow patrons bought him drink after drink, lining them up in front of him in ridiculous numbers, surpassing the limits of what any man could consume. Sometimes he drove or rode with friends over to Wasilla and stopped at the Wasilla Bar, Hallea Lodge, or Green Acres for a few drinks. If he was riding with someone and the conversation took a turn for the worse or an argument ensued, he might employ his standard "hang it in your ear," or words to that effect, and refuse a ride home with the offending party. If Dr. Hume became too irritable to be around, sometimes people just left him. He wasn't overly concerned about that; he would just drift off to hang out with other customers, knowing that someone would always be happy to give the doctor a ride home. The next time he encountered a friend who had stranded him, nothing much, if anything, was said about the incident. He held no grudges. A rather extreme illustration of this involved his friend Al Ose. Dr. Hume and Ose were traveling back from Anchorage when a heated verbal altercation erupted in the vicinity of the Knik River bridge. The doctor pulled the car over and told Ose to get out. Ose said that someone was leaving the car, but it wasn't going to be him. With that, he reached across the doctor, opened the driver's side door, and pushed Dr. Hume out of the car. Sliding behind the wheel, Ose took off for Palmer in the doctor's car. The next time the pair met up, and in subsequent meetings, they laughed off the whole thing.

Sometimes when the doctor was out and about, something would trigger a memory from the past and he would act on the recollection. Once, while attending a Saturday night function that featured live music, he requested a song and phoned his sister Doreen. When she answered, he cued the band and they launched into *The Yellow Rose of Texas* and the doctor held the phone so she could listen. At times, he called and talked to old girlfriends.

He still shot a lot of pool, but to make the games a little more interesting he began playing for money. He also gambled on shuffleboard and cribbage.

One unheralded aspect of his nighttime socializing was his unfailing generosity. Through his profession, he was already greatly aware of who needed help in the community. To these persons he provided much assistance through unbilled medical services. But on the town, he learned of still others who needed a hand. He helped people anonymously, often in concert with his close friend Neal Wright, who was also an amazingly generous individual. If Neal got wind of a need, he would report it to the doctor or vice versa. When a local family's home sustained extensive fire damage, the doctor and Neal bought them a washer and dryer and had it delivered without fanfare. The doctor gave people money outright and loaned it too, with no expectations of a payback. When he saw a local college student, John Maze, still working after the school year had begun, he asked the young man why he had not gone back to college. Maze reported that he couldn't afford to return for the fall semester, so he was working and saving for the spring session. With the promise that he would attend fall classes, Dr. Hume wrote Maze a $1,000 check on the spot, to cover his expenses.

The Home Front

The Hume children were growing up. The three eldest girls were bright, cute, and vivacious. April was the larger than life one of the bunch. She was gorgeous, exceptionally smart, and outspoken. Brimming with self-confidence, she seemed fearless in any academic or social situation. Dawn was a beauty in her own right and an outstanding student, but was more introspective than April and lacked some of her older sister's self-assuredness. For Cindy, the girlish interests of April and Dawn seemed a mystery. She wondered how anyone could care about all that feminine stuff when opportunities for adventure with the guys were in the offing. Most of those adventures were undertaken with her brother Frank, with whom she shared a close relationship. Frank was an outdoorsy kid and good in school too, though he did not exhibit the overachieving ways of his siblings. Frank thought other things in life were just as important as schoolwork. Starr, so much younger than the rest, was something of the family mascot. But she too was pretty and an ace student. All of these attributes, the physical attractiveness, the high intelligence, and the fact that they were the children of a doctor would seem to be components of small town royalty. But it didn't play like that; all the Hume children were immensely approachable, friendly, and popular with their peers.

A significant portion of the children's positive behavior could be traced to the lessons in discipline, responsibility, and respect they learned at home. As children and young adults, their focus was primarily on schoolwork. They were expected to complete their homework in a timely manner without a lot of assistance. In addition to schoolwork, the kids were expected to help around the house. April, Dawn, and Cindy rotated on dishwashing and other duties. Frank emptied the trash, and during the winter months shoveled the walk. Their allowance, fifty cents a week, was tied to their labors. For a large family living in a relatively small space, they got along well, owed in part to the mutual respect their parents advocated. Most of the parental guidance was supplied by Myrt in the doctor's absence, but he observed enough of his children's behavior to realize that Myrt was keeping them right on track. More or less passing through their lives, the doctor's approach to childrearing was more liberal than his wife's, and he was a much easier touch when it came to granting the children permission to undertake outside interests. He harbored little concern that his children's activities would put them at peril or that he or Myrt would not know of their whereabouts; the children were far too trustworthy for that. Besides, he knew that after his generous permissiveness, Myrt would quickly restore order in the wake of his imminent departure.

The relationship between Dr. Hume and Myrt was exceedingly complex. Far too many things had been left unsaid and undone, just as too many hurtful things had been said and done. Past offenses had little time to heal while still more transgressions, on the same old themes, were regularly committed. Even in the aftermath of 1964 Alaska earthquake—at 9.2 on the Richter scale, the most powerful quake ever recorded in U.S. history—the doctor remained at a local bar for hours before returning home to his family. This, like many other offenses, seemed so clearly avoidable. It made for an almost palpable sense of underlying tension, despite the fact that they still loved each other very much. The doctor even said so. Countless times he told his friends and co-workers about his love for his wife and family, speaking of Myrt's strength as a wife and a mother, and singling out the children individually to describe their most positive qualities.

Often the doctor demonstrated his love through gift giving. He put considerable thought into gift selections. One year for Christmas he gave his wife gold, frankincense, and myrrh. Another time he gave her a toolbox full of tools, his subtle tip of the hat to her for running the household on her own. Once, after a huge argument, he bought her a Cadillac. He didn't care about material wealth for himself; its only value was in giving to the ones he loved.

As a couple, the Humes escaped for dinner from time to time to Anchorage hotspots like the Rabbit Creek Inn or The Rice Bowl. Any place that served alcohol had potential for putting the evening at risk, but observers noticed that with his wife around, the doctor's drinking was at its most restrained. Sometimes, with all the chaos that swirled around them, even the simplest of outings could prove to be unnerving. On one occasion the doctor piloted his plane to Talkeetna to provide medical services. Once there, and before he went to work, he phoned Myrt and asked if she wanted to join him on a fishing expedition after he had finished for the day. Myrt thought the idea sounded fun. She drove to the Wasilla Railroad Station and boarded a train for Talkeetna. Upon arrival, she was met by her husband and the two made their way to the river's edge where a boat and pilot waited to take them fishing. Soon after leaving shore, it became obvious that the pilot was drunk. The next realization was that the water was running too fast and high for fishing. The icy water was brown with silt and full of debris. Next, the boat engine died. The pilot was having difficulties restarting it. They were floating out of control. At that point the doctor leaned over to his wife and suggested she slip out of her boots in the event the boat swamped and they all ended up in the water. Finally the motor was started and they made it safely back to shore, another narrow escape.

Despite their roller coaster ride of a marriage, they stayed together, and even added another family member with the birth of their last child, John. The doctor knew he had married a rock solid woman. He could not find another like her, and he knew it. More than a few people wondered why Myrt stayed with him, but Myrt knew a different man than they did; she knew Vince before he became a doctor and before the start of his heavy drinking.

Cases in the Practice

Dr. Hume's hospital and home office medical practice remained brisk. A few positive changes had been made at the hospital. A rotating on-call schedule was finally established for doctors at the emergency room. Gone were the days when ER doctors only treated their private practice patients. His office nurse, Jessie DeVries, left his employ, and went to work at the hospital. Penny Busby took over the office nursing duties, and Elayne Williams continued her role as receptionist. As with any general medical practice, the cases Dr. Hume handled ran from the typical to the bizarre.

Being called upon after hours at home continued to be a source of irritation. One evening as the late night television news was wrapping up, a knock came on the Hume's residence door. Myrt opened the door to find a man standing with his teenage daughter. The girl looked to be under some anxiety. The man said his daughter had "a bellyache" accompanied by some "female type problems." Myrt reported this to the doctor who said he would see the girl as soon as the news was over. He told Myrt to prep her for an examination. Before the doctor could make his way downstairs, Myrt was back to tell him the girl was going to have a baby, and it didn't appear that it would be long in coming. She was right; they all arrived at the hospital just in time. The doctor helped the terrified, completely unprepared, young girl through labor and delivery of the baby. He also provided guidance to her stunned father, who had been altogether unaware his daughter was pregnant. On that particular night, his counseling services were probably more needed than his medical abilities.

Dr. Hume had extended office hours one night a week, for those who could not take time from work for a doctor's visit. One of those nights, a truck driver came in with a pilonidal abscess, an infected cyst at the bottom of the tailbone. The cyst was very large and filled with pus. The man was in quite a bit of pain, which had been exacerbated by his sitting on the cyst for long periods while driving. Dr. Hume lanced the cyst and the pressure from within propelled a stream of pus with such force that it splattered the ceiling and made a reeking mess of the exam table and floor. The man was much relieved and went away happy. So much for the lofty status of being a doctor, and even more so, the lofty status of being the doctor's wife as Myrt, armed with Clorox, performed clean up, floor to ceiling.

Another time, a man came in with an injury that Dr. Hume said was best treated with a shot. The man protested, saying he didn't want a shot because he was on the wagon. The doctor explained, with a twinkle in his eye, that he was thinking of an inoculation rather than an adult beverage.

Because he kept up on the latest medical advances, Dr. Hume recognized when a local boy with a serious heart condition would benefit from out-of-state treatment through a brand new procedure. The family involved was without the funds or wherewithal to coordinate the whole business, which included the acquisition of sixteen pints of blood needed for the open-heart surgery. Dr. Hume arranged it all for them.

He had a number of unusual emergency room visits too. One was complicated by a power outage. A man was admitted for treatment with severe bleeding from his nose that required stitches. Just when Dr. Hume was about to begin his work, the lights went out, which sent the nurses scrambling for flashlights. He placed each stitch by the light of handheld flashlights, no small order because of shadow, glare, and a dubious patient. While he worked he smiled, shook his head, and said, "Strange days."

He remained close to his patients and their families. When

a local couple brought in their two sons for diagnosis and treatment, the doctor became concerned. Both boys bruised very easily; just a light touch could bring on swelling and discoloration. The doctor examined the boys and then educated the parents on the possible causes of the extreme reactions to touch. Among those possibilities was a rare inherited disease, his initial diagnosis. He thought the situation was serious and recommended they seek further advice from a specialist. The parents did as instructed and visited a specialist in Anchorage who had been briefed by Dr. Hume. When the father of the boys reported the specialist's findings and a less serious diagnosis back to Dr. Hume, he displayed such sincere relief that it touched the boys' father. With no reaction to being "overruled," Dr. Hume seemed to care about the boys as if they were his own.

The way the doctor balanced the emotional and healthcare needs of one woman who had given birth to a baby with a severe, and ultimately fatal, birth defect was significant. After delivering the baby, he gave the first time mother the terrible news about the infant's condition and assured her that she was not at fault. He then called Dr. Helen Whaley of Anchorage, asking her to lend support in the delicate matter. Dr. Whaley caught a flight to Palmer. She consoled the woman, confirmed that she was not the cause of the birth defect, and told her she should not be afraid to have another baby. The woman had never seen a female doctor before, and she found real comfort in Dr. Whaley's care, just as Dr. Hume thought she would. Later, a Catholic priest looked in on the mother, one of his parishioners, and offered advice and solace. The priest told her that he had baptized her baby, and that made her feel better. In fact, he said, the baby was baptized twice. "Baptized twice?" she said in surprise. "Yes," said the priest, "Dr. Hume, fearing I wouldn't get here in time, baptized him right after he was born."

The Highway Blues

At 2:30 A.M. on May 24, 1964, a nurse at Valley Presbyterian Hospital placed a call to the Hume residence requesting that the doctor report to the emergency room. A motor vehicle accident had occurred at Mile 53 on the Glenn Highway, and an ambulance was already on-site picking up the injured parties. The nurse reported that the injuries were serious, and it wouldn't be long before the ambulance would arrive at the hospital. Myrt had answered the phone, and after hearing the nurse's request, suggested she call another doctor as her husband was at the Alpine Inn in Sutton and wouldn't be available to take the call.

Indeed Dr. Hume had been at the Alpine Inn. He arrived at about 10:00 P.M. on the evening of the 23rd and ordered a beer. The owner of the establishment saw him at the bar and asked what had brought him to Sutton. The doctor said he was there to attend the miners' picnic that was taking place across the highway. The two engaged in some good-natured banter on how it was that Dr. Hume considered himself a miner. After the doctor had finished his drink, he and the bar owner got into the doctor's 1962 Ford four-wheel drive pickup and drove over to the picnic. Even at that relatively late picnicking hour, a lot of food and beer was still available. Dr. Hume stayed at the picnic for about two hours then returned to the Alpine Inn for a nightcap before heading back to Palmer. The doctor had been on the highway for perhaps only a minute when, after crossing the Eska Creek bridge, he lost control of the big Ford and veered into oncoming traffic running a car off the road. The driver of the car took to the ditch, but in a short distance was able to regain the road. One of the three passengers in the sedan cried out, "I think that was Doc Hume, and he's going to wreck before he gets to Palmer."

Dr. Hume drove about eight more miles to the area of Buffalo Mine Road, where he once again crossed over the centerline in the presence of oncoming traffic. That's when he encountered seventeen-year-old Mark Moffitt who was behind the wheel of his 1955 Chrysler Windsor. Jack Corey was a passenger in the Moffitt car. Moffitt took evasive action, but it was too late—the three-quarter ton pickup slammed into the sedan in a horrendous head-on and sideswiping motion. The impact sent Moffitt through the windshield, breaking his left leg on the steering wheel as he exited the car. The Windsor rolled over, coming to rest on its top. One-hundred-nineteen feet away, the pickup came to a stop. Within minutes, two separate motorists came upon the scene of the accident. The Windsor had obviously sustained the most damage, so the motorists inspected that wreckage first, correctly assuming that was the area of greatest need. They found Moffitt on the ground moaning in pain, his head and face bleeding, his leg askew from his body. Jack Corey was standing nearby, dazed. One of the motorists went for help, the other stayed at the scene directing traffic. Several drivers stopped to ask if they might be of service. Two were sent to summon help. The motorist left at the scene began moving toward the pickup, removing accident debris from the highway as he walked. That's when he met Dr. Hume, himself dazed and bleeding from the nose, walking in the direction of the Windsor. Both men walked back to the Moffitt car. The doctor set about examining both Moffitt and Corey. He ascertained that Moffitt had a broken femur, a compound fracture, and lacerations about the head. Corey had abrasions to his head and bruising to his face, shoulder, and chest. A light drizzle was falling and the doctor covered the young men with blankets.

A member of the Alaska State Police responded to the scene, asked questions, and checked on Moffitt's condition. Dr. Hume asked the policeman to leave the boy alone, stating that he would be all right and that an ambulance was en route. When the policeman asked for his driver's license, Dr. Hume became agitated, and the two had words before he eventually surrendered it. From his observations of the doctor's speech, general conduct, and the strong smell of alcohol, the policeman made notations concerning the doctor's level of inebriation. When the ambulance arrived, an attendant bent over Moffitt to check if he could be moved in a safe manner, and the doctor grabbed him and told him the boy would be okay. The attendant then asked the doctor about his own condition and he responded only that he "was in a real mess." As Moffitt was being placed on a stretcher the doctor tried to help, but nearly fell on the boy in the process. Finally, with all three of the injured parties loaded into the ambulance, the emergency vehicle took off for Palmer. On the four-mile trip to town, Dr. Hume slouched down in his ambulance seat and napped.

When the ambulance arrived at the hospital, the doctor who had been summoned was surprised to see Dr. Hume walking through the emergency room doors. From the dried blood on his shirt, he assumed Dr. Hume had been in the accident too and asked him if he was okay. Dr. Hume said yes and went about taking charge of the situation, ordering x-rays for Moffitt and care for Corey. Upon hearing that his assistance would not be required, the other doctor left. The injuries to Mark Moffitt were as noted at the scene, but with better lighting at the hospital it was also apparent that his impact with the older vehicle's non-tempered windshield had left him with a substantial amount of glass in his scalp as well as in his eyes. After an overnight stay in Palmer, he was transported to Providence Hospital in Anchorage for further care.

Moffitt's insurance company sued the doctor, and a cash settlement was reached. The State of Alaska pursued reckless driving charges against Dr. Hume for which he entered a plea of guilty. He was given a $300 fine with $100 suspended, and no jail time. The "real mess" Dr. Hume had envisioned for himself while at the accident scene never materialized.

The South Seas

Myrt and the children had taken a lengthy driving vacation a couple years earlier; now it was time for husband and wife to get away. Originally, the doctor intended to take in a medical convention in Australia with a vacation on the side, but the convention dates were misinterpreted and the trip turned into a straight vacation. The journey was extensive. They visited Tokyo, Singapore, Hong Kong, New Zealand, Australia, and Fiji. Near Korolevu, Fiji, a photography team was working on an advertising campaign for Qantas Airlines when they spotted Myrt. The team approached her and asked if she might be willing to participate as a model in the shoot. When she agreed to pose for them, they asked her how much she wanted in compensation. She really didn't know what an appropriate amount was, so after a minute she suggested the team cover the cost of a long distance phone call back to Alaska so she could talk to her children. The team readily accepted. The shoot was productive, and one of the photographs was selected for use in the ad campaign. The photo featured Myrt seated on a woven grass mat, attired in a floral print dress with flowers in her hair. She was surrounded by five smiling Native islanders catering to her with gifts of food, pineapples, coconuts, and bananas. The subjects were set against a backdrop of palm trees and a great bamboo grass hut. Myrt's big smile had a slightly quizzical look to it, her arms outstretched in front of her, palms up, gave the impression that she was thinking, "Is all this for me?" The caption below the image read, "All I said was Qantas." The photo fit perfectly into the advertising campaign's design to impress on the consumer that Qantas travelers were distinctive individuals, fitting of special treatment. The full-page ad appeared in *Time*, *Newsweek,* and *Sunset* magazines and was the subject of travel posters as well.

Posing for the Qantas ad. (*Hume family collection*)

The Humes had a good vacation, but it was marred by an intense argument that centered on the doctor's heavy drinking. One night Myrt awoke to find the doctor gone. She didn't know where he could be and began to worry he had taken a nighttime swim in potentially-dangerous tide waters. In her concern, she alerted some fellow travelers. The doctor eventually returned to the room, and it was apparent he had been drinking. The two quarreled and the doctor left in anger. The next day when he returned, he found that Myrt was preparing to go back to Alaska on her own. After a heated discussion, he asked what he could do that would make her stay until the end of the trip so they could return home together. Myrt's demands were simple: have a meal, go to bed, and don't drink anymore during the vacation. Dr. Hume agreed, but for him the parameters of the vacation were something of a gray area; did the plane ride back *really* count as part of the vacation? As he often did, he saw a caveat to the promise he had made, and on the long flight home, he drank heavily. In Seattle the doctor took a flight to British Columbia to visit his father, while Myrt returned to Alaska alone.

Back to Overwork

Alaska in general and Palmer in particular had long experienced a problem with recruiting doctors. Remoteness, coupled with the perception of backward, primitive facilities did not appeal to doctors trying to build a practice. For a short period of time, Palmer had actually been rich with physicians when Drs. Skille, Bailey, Hume, and Colberg were joined by Dr. Cunningham, but there wasn't enough business for five doctors, and little by little most of them left the area. By the early summer of 1965, when Dr. Bailey departed for Arizona, only two physicians remained—Dr. Hume and Dr. Cunningham. Although there wasn't enough work for five doctors, there was way too much for two.

The shortage of doctors was no secret. It was a subject often discussed at hospital board meetings, where concern was expressed that if adequate physician coverage could not be maintained, the hospital would have to close its doors. The discussion was conducted in wider public forums too. *The Frontiersman* newspaper carried a number of stories reporting on the arduous workload the doctors were facing. In response to the problem, a committee was formed to explore possible solutions. The committee worked to involve borough and city government, local organizations and clubs, as well as individual citizens in what was termed an "all-out advertising campaign" to lure doctors north. Try as they might to sell the merits of the community, nothing seemed to work.

Mary Beth

Many of Dr. Hume's patients had a profound emotional impact on him, but perhaps none more so than two-year-old Mary Beth Bouwens. On her family's farm, one of Mary Beth's legs became entangled in the machinery of an operating commercial fertilizer spreader, an unimaginably horrendous accident. Her leg was severely mangled, virtually missing altogether below the knee. It was immediately plain there would be no saving her leg—the only hope was in saving her life. Mary Beth's father, Wayne, gathered up his badly bleeding daughter, wrapped her leg in a blanket, and placed a call to Dr. Hume. Wayne reported he was headed for the hospital with Mary Beth, and he quickly explained the extent of her injuries. On the way, Wayne exhorted his daughter to keep talking, crying, anything to keep her conscious and alive until he could get her to Dr. Hume. After talking with the father by phone, Dr. Hume immediately called local pilot Buddy Woods, putting him on alert that his services would likely be required for an emergency flight to Anchorage.

When Wayne pulled up to the emergency room entrance, he found Dr. Hume standing outside waiting for him. The doctor rushed the little girl inside to examine her. After stabilizing Mary Beth, he came out and told her father simply, "We're going to Anchorage." He called the already prepared pilot and confirmed that he would be needed, then he telephoned Dr. Mills in Anchorage to request preparations for immediate surgery. On the flight, Dr. Hume held the little girl in his arms while he managed a tourniquet. When they touched down at Merrill Field, an ambulance was waiting to take them to Providence Hospital, where Dr. Mills was standing by. Dr. Hume assisted during surgery. In addition to performing an amputation of the lower leg, they were successful in saving Mary Beth's knee, so important for her future mobility. Following surgery, Dr. Hume was offered transportation back to Palmer, but he declined the ride in favor of staying through the night with the little girl. Satisfied with her progress, he returned home the following day. In telling his wife of Mary Beth's ordeal, Dr. Hume was overcome with emotion, finally breaking down and crying on Myrt's shoulder for the better part of an hour.

Getting away from it all at a hunting camp at Boulder Creek, Alaska. From left Dr. Simons, Vern Marple, and Dr. Hume. (*Lucas family collection*)

The Beginning of the End

The burden of incessant work, the pressure to perform, and the emotional strain he experienced from close relationships with his patients continued without letup, except for those brief periods when he got out of town altogether. One of those out-of-town excursions placed Dr. Hume on the Alaska Highway during the cold winter of 1965. He intended to be home for Christmas, motoring north on December 23rd when, in the vicinity of Haines Junction, he crested a hill and discovered a southbound pickup with a camper in his lane. Without time to take defensive action, he collided head-on with the other vehicle. The impact sent the doctor's car down a steep embankment. As a result of front end body damage, he was unable to open the car's front doors and was forced instead to crawl into the back seat of the car, where he put on extra clothing and crawled out a back door. After all the serious motor vehicle accidents in which Dr. Hume had escaped injury, he literally couldn't walk away from this one. He was forced to scale the embankment by pulling himself up by his arms. After he reached the roadway, he struggled over to the driver of the pickup truck. The man had sustained a head injury, which was rapidly becoming an emergency situation. The temperature had dropped to a frigid forty degrees below zero. Fortunately, the doctor had thought to grab a flashlight, which he used to hail passing motorists. The two men were eventually rescued, and Dr. Hume was transported to Whitehorse General Hospital. Myrt was unable to book a flight to join him in Whitehorse, but John Hume came up from Vancouver to be with his son. Dr. Hume stayed at the hospital for four days, missing Christmas at home. The x-rays revealed a fractured right hip and a broken left ankle. From Whitehorse, he and his father took a flight to Alaska. Upon deplaning in Anchorage, Dr. Hume was transported to Providence Hospital, where he stayed for another eight days. Finally he was allowed to return to Palmer, overnighting at Valley Presbyterian Hospital before going home.

Dr. Hume's period of convalescence was frustrating, very painful, and slow—too slow for a normal recovery. After a time the doctor began to suspect he had a bone infection. He mentioned the possibility to his Anchorage physician who disagreed with his self-diagnosis. But Dr. Hume was correct; a bone in his hip had become infected. Pus from the infection resulted in an abscess that deprived the bone of adequate blood supply, leaving him with dead bone tissue and a chronic infection. The dead tissue needed to be removed and replaced with a bone graft. This procedure was best undertaken out-of-state, so Dr. Hume flew to Utah for an autograft operation. After the dead bone tissue was eliminated, a section of his own healthy bone was shaped to fit the space, and then inserted and held in place with plates and screws. Complications arose when excessive bleeding required several blood transfusions. Following a period of recovery in the Utah hospital, Dr. Hume was allowed to return home to restart his convalescence.

He found recovery at home, once again, to be frustrating. He wasn't used to the home environment, he wasn't able to hit his nighttime haunts, and perhaps worst of all, he couldn't work. At least his children got to know him a little better while he was housebound. Sometimes he wasn't much fun to be around, as he was antsy and a little nasty as a result of his confinement. But there were times when he reached out to his family. One night as his daughter Dawn prepared for a date, he said, "If you come home early enough, we can watch a movie together on TV." It was a casual offer, but an offer nonetheless, and Dawn made certain she was home in time to watch the movie with her father.

Dr. Hume on crutches. Myrt was only slightly taller than her husband. Here, it should be noted, she is standing on a step next to him. (*Hume family collection*)

When Dr. Hume finally started to get around on crutches, his mobility was still quite limited. He had to be driven around, doors had to be opened for him, and special allowances made, all of which severely reduced his independence. He remained in serious discomfort and took Percodan to relieve the pain. He took the highly habit-forming yellow tablets for an extended period of time, risky in itself but even more so for an individual with a history of alcohol abuse.

Cases While on Crutches

During Dr. Hume's long convalescence, Dr. Edwin Kraft handled patients in the basement office. Finally, though still on crutches, Dr. Hume returned to his practice. Getting around his own office wasn't so bad, but venturing outside of the home for work proved problematic. The need for his services, however, would not wait for his full recovery.

In the beginning, Myrt assumed the role of her husband's

chauffeur, and though she had few illusions as to the nature of his work, the experience was nonetheless an eye opener. One night, the doctor was summoned by the Palmer Police to a private residence where a murder had been committed. Myrt drove the doctor to the house and carried his medical bag inside while he hobbled behind on crutches. Inside the house, they were directed to a bedroom, the actual scene of the crime. On their way to the bedroom, the Humes passed a man, the victim's husband and prime suspect, talking with police. Myrt entered the bedroom and saw the carnage—the lady of the house lying across her bed, victim of a gunshot. Myrt put down her husband's bag and beat a hasty retreat outside for air. The doctor carried out the duties for which he was summoned and pronounced the woman dead. As soon as he had finished his work at the murder scene, an urgent request was delivered for Dr. Hume to report to the hospital. Myrt drove him to the hospital and helped him inside the building. The doctor was ready to work when an ambulance arrived at the emergency room entrance. Myrt, standing nearby, witnessed a terribly ashen-faced heart attack victim being wheeled into the emergency room to receive care from her husband. Again, she excused herself to go outside. Myrt composed herself and wondered how her husband could withstand the onslaught of such pain and suffering on a regular basis.

Dr. Hume still experienced enormous difficulty dealing with human suffering. When a local man whom the doctor knew and respected was stricken with cancer and eventually succumbed to the disease, Dr. Hume was distressed that not only was he unable to affect a cure, but he was also unsuccessful in relieving the man's or his family's suffering. Intellectually he understood the limitations of modern medicine, but emotionally, the tremendous gulf between what was actually needed and what he could perform was discouraging.

The results of the car accident, infection, bone graft, and chronic pain made Dr. Hume's job harder, but took nothing from his effectiveness. He was still making an important difference in the small community. In addition to treating the usual day-to-day colds, flu, and allergies, he skillfully stitched up deep cuts that healed with little scarring. He successfully rebuilt the hands of a number of people who had been told they would forever have limited function. He loved a challenge and others in his profession knew it, for he received a number of "hopeless" or "unwanted" case referrals. One of those cases involved a morbidly obese Anchorage man in need of a gall-bladder operation. Of the Anchorage physicians the man had visited, no one was interested in performing the procedure. Some suggested he venture north to Palmer for a visit with Dr. Hume. As expected, Dr. Hume took the case and successfully performed the operation. Knowing that an extended hospital stay was beyond the man's financial reach, Dr. Hume allowed him to convalesce in the basement office, even providing him meals during his stay. When sufficiently recovered, the man returned to Anchorage, leaving the Hume's basement a foul mess and the entirety of his medical bill unpaid. The episode was annoying, but the doctor didn't bemoan it or pursue the matter monetarily.

He wasn't out of miracles yet either. When a mother called Dr. Hume's office to ask about home treatment for her young son's flu-like symptoms, the doctor took particular interest in the boy's ailment. He recommended an office visit. The woman politely demurred, stating it was probably just the flu—certainly nothing to be overly concerned about. The doctor strongly recommended an office visit, relating that he was troubled by the described symptoms, which might indicate a problem with his appendix. The woman brought her son in at once and discovered he was suffering from appendicitis, for which he underwent a prompt operation and fully recovered. Without Dr. Hume's insight, it could have developed into a serious emergency.

Another case involved a local high school youth who just barely made it to the hospital under his own power before losing consciousness. He regained consciousness for only a short time before his condition worsened, and he lapsed into a coma. From that point his health rapidly declined. No one could figure out what was wrong with him. Soon his kidneys were failing too. Some staff members suggested he be flown out-of-state for care, but others thought it was too late for that and he would not survive the trip. Dr. Hume thought the answer to the young man's ailment might be found in his habits or lifestyle. The doctor started calling the boy's friends to find out what he had been doing in the hours, days, and weeks prior to his hospitalization. Employing these investigative methods, Dr. Hume learned the boy hadn't been doing anything out of the ordinary, just preparing his car to be painted. The doctor seized upon this information. What kind of compounds or solvents was the teen using to prep the metal surface? The answer was found in the garage where he had been working—a tin of a heavy colorless liquid used as a grease removing agent. This substance, later banned, presented a number of health risks if inhaled or even touched. With this knowledge, a treatment plan was devised, and he too made a full recovery.

Scores of other medical cases during this period illustrated Dr. Hume's continued compassion for those who came to him for treatment. One little girl had scoliosis and needed physical therapy. Concerned that she might be sensitive about the problem, Dr. Hume contacted the school district's physical therapist, who was roving throughout the schools conducting talks and exercise clinics for JFK's Physical Fitness Program. He explained the girl's needs to the therapist and from that point on the child was always picked to "volunteer" to demonstrate an exercise to her schoolmates that had surreptitiously been designed just for her. She loved the attention, and always felt special when she was chosen. She was also willing to practice the exercises at home that she learned while assisting in the demonstrations. It was just what the doctor ordered.

He had other ways of providing care for young people too, never missing an opportunity to counsel when it was needed. This was particularly true for young boys who required treatment because of fighting. While they were a captive audience, Dr. Hume, in no uncertain terms, let them know his thoughts on physical aggression. The boys sometimes referred to it as "hardass counseling," but Dr. Hume was a man worthy of respect, so they listened and knew he was right.

While he generally displayed a self-confident, even gutsy, approach to medicine, he was often measured in his methods too. When a young girl who had swallowed a pin was brought to see Dr. Hume, he suggested a non-intrusive method of handling the situation by simply tracking the object via x-rays, allowing the body a chance to pass the pin naturally. Her parents had expected a more immediate approach, but they agreed to give the proposal a try and the pin passed without need for surgery.

Throughout the time Dr. Hume was on crutches, he maintained the hallmarks of his private practice: his amazing gifts in diagnosis and healing, his dedication to his patients, and his seemingly tireless approach to his work. However, he also grew more unpredictable in his professional relationships. He was much more likely now to dress down a nurse for a mistake or oversight, often in front of other staff or even patients. He uttered outrageous comments, presumably for the sake of shock value. He lashed out in frustration, too. A Sunday afternoon emergency room call brought him to the hospital to treat a woman who complained of being ill with fever. He examined her and found nothing amiss. Her body temperature was normal. That seemed to push him over the edge; he took the thermometer and threw it hard across the room and left the hospital. To the nurse his actions said, don't call me on a Sunday to treat a patient with fever unless she *has* a fever, and to the woman his message was don't waste my time with foolishness.

Sometimes a justifiable outburst, so seemingly in the offing, never materialized. Another emergency room callout found the doctor placing stitches in a man who had suffered a number of deep lacerations. From almost the beginning of the procedure, the man speechified about his faith, and how his trust in God had always provided him everything he had ever really needed. The doctor, concentrating on his work, looked up from time to time to nod. The man continued on about how everyone should put his trust in God, and how it would be a better world if everyone did. Finally, near the end of his treatment, the man got around to mentioning that the doctor should also put his trust in God, because then he would understand and accept the fact that he would not be paid for the emergency room visit. The nurses braced themselves for an angry eruption that never came; the doctor was not in the least bit perturbed. He had become so unpredictable that the nurses never knew what they were getting when they called Dr. Hume.

A Summer Place

Dr. Hume's hip pain became chronic. More than a year had passed since his December, 1965 auto accident, and he was still suffering and still on crutches. The Percodan relieved the pain, but he was keenly aware of the risks of prolonged use of the drug. In addition to its highly addictive qualities, long-term procurement of the drug caused others to be at risk too, for although Dr. Hume possessed a narcotics license, he was prohibited from writing prescriptions for his own use. Of course the doctor had close friends in the business who could make drugs available to him, but, again, there were sizable risks entailed. Something had to give.

In July, 1967 the doctor turned over his practice, his office, and his log home for the remainder of the summer to Dr. Thomas Green. The Humes took up residence at their Finger Lake house for some needed rest. The lake house had long been the place where the doctor was most at ease, where he was less likely to be intruded upon, and where his practice cast less of a shadow on his personal life. It was a place of recreation: fishing, hunting, golfing, and double handed bridge. The alcoholic beverages offered at Barry's Resort were nearby too, though overall he drank less while at the lake house. But that leisurely summer was not to be enjoyed by Dr. Hume at his lake house for long; pain and immobility persisted. Before long, he decided he needed to go to Richmond, Virginia, for extensive physical rehabilitation.

Meanwhile Back at the Hospital

The emotions regarding Dr. Hume's summer hiatus were decidedly mixed at the hospital. The confidence the nurses had in his medical abilities was well intact, but some had misgivings about his increased lack of professionalism. His loose and sometimes vulgar talk was upsetting. He often showed up red-eyed and disheveled, which ran counter to the ideal of cleanliness they had adopted in nursing school. Numerous awful stories were circulating about him downtown, stories that shed a bad light on the medical profession in general and on the hospital in particular. A number of the nurses were concerned about their own roles in it all. They discussed how some nurses had helped him with the medical oxygen in an effort to get him sober, or had sometimes looked away and pretended he wasn't inebriated. They wondered about their culpability in such situations. Some of the talk was driven by hurt feelings and grudges from past personal conflicts with the doctor. But a lot of the conversations were issue-based. The discussions varied from the personal to the professional, and nearly every-one seemed to have an illustrative story about him, but even those varied widely. Some nurses talked of drunkenness while others had never seen him drunk, even once. Even those who worked with him most closely were unable to reach any kind of consensus on what should be done, if anything, about Dr. Hume. But for several of the nurses, the solution was clear. For them, the days of making excuses for him were over.

12

What to do About Dr. Hume

The Tipping Point

For a protracted period, the hospital board of directors' time and energy had been monopolized by two issues: meeting the financial challenges of the hospital, and resolving the personnel matters of Dr. Hume. During the summer of 1967 while Dr. Hume was away, the discussions intensified. Under provisions of the bylaws, the board entered into private executive sessions. There they discussed the concept of a doctor's privileges in serving at the hospital. The focus of the talks turned to how to motivate Dr. Hume to be respectful of his privileges. Dr. Hume was well aware of the board's ongoing concerns regarding his drinking, his privileges had been suspended in 1962, and he had been sued by Frances Schupp, all of which had made no lasting change in his behavior. The word "potential" was used over and over in the board's discussions about Dr. Hume. There was the potential for lawsuits. Also, the church had made it known that it didn't condone the goings-on at the hospital, so there was potential that an important funding source could be lost. There was the potential for the loss of insurance on the facility. In all, there was a very real potential of losing the entire hospital because of the actions of one man—one man and a potentially culpable board of directors who had allowed it to happen. Additionally, the board members had a level of personal liability if they did not correct a problem about which they had knowledge. They could attempt to deny responsibility with a claim that the board had been involved with the big picture of running the hospital, with little knowledge of the day-to-day operation, and that was generally true, except in this case. Many citizens, organizations, and employees had come forward, and so many stories had circulated in the community regarding the doctor's overuse of alcohol that plausible deniability was not a credible excuse for lack of action. They knew that they and previous boards had been enablers of a sort, allowing the situation to continue and even escalate.

In the administrative chain of events that finally led to a decisive action in the matter of Dr. Hume, one event was critical. A nurse addressed the hospital board in executive session and, permitted to speak freely, laid out a list of complaints against the doctor that were backed up with supporting documentation. The chief grievance was that the doctor regularly worked while under the influence of alcohol. She told them that a number of nurses genuinely feared for their personal safety when he was drunk. She said that patients were at risk because of Dr. Hume's inconsistent recordkeeping when he was inebriated. She expressed concern about the accuracy of his prescription-writing while he was under the influence. She bore a wealth of anecdotal information about emergency room calls that were not responded to, and scheduled medical procedures that did not take place, accompanied by dates, times, and the parties involved. She spoke of his delivering babies while he was drunk and about how the nurses deftly tried to get the newborns away from him as soon as possible, fearing he would drop them. She admitted that Dr. Hume was "on to" their efforts in this regard and would lash out at them with a torrent of obscenities when they tried to intervene. She acknowledged, too, that the doctor's skills were formidable and respected by the staff. She said that no one had been harmed by Dr. Hume to date. But it was clear, she said, that his problem with alcohol, and perhaps with painkillers, was progressive. Eventually these substances would have an even more profound effect on his ability to make decisions and perform his duties. The dangers associated with Dr. Hume's continued practice at the hospital could no longer be termed as potential, they had become probable. The nurse had done her homework. Her testimony was direct, well-documented, and persuasive. She presented factual evidence that was difficult to refute and impossible to ignore.

Reaching accord on the action to be taken required much group discussion and personal soul-searching by the board members. Their responsibilities to the hospital and the community were clear, but they still held great respect for Dr. Hume's remarkable skills and compassion. Besides, for a majority of the board members, he was their trusted family physician. Past boards had deferred this decision for a variety of reasons: board terms were offset, which allowed a changing level of tolerance for the situation; the state of affairs arguably had not yet reached a critical level; and perhaps previous boards just were not up to the task of undertaking such a controversial action. But the time had undeniably come to resolve the matter, and the board of directors in place was a particularly strong group, confident in its measured approach in deciding the proper personnel action. When the motion was made and seconded and the votes were tallied, the board voted overwhelmingly to suspend Dr. Hume's hospital privileges.

The board did not take immediate action on its decision, hoping to first shore-up support from within the medical community. But no such support was forthcoming, and in short order the board realized it would have to go the administrative action alone. Board members were all keenly aware of the controversial nature of suspending the popular doctor, but they did not foresee the great tidal wave of public support for Dr. Hume, or the pressure they were about to endure.

The Missed Call

An unsuspecting Dr. Hume returned to Alaska from his summer stay in Virginia much improved physically. His rehabilitation had been augmented with daily swims which put him back on his feet. The crutches he had relied upon for more than a year were gone, though he still walked with a slight limp. Nevertheless, it was an impressive recovery, and Dr. Hume seemed rejuvenated to return to work, which he did on September 6th, once again seeing patients in his basement office. Going back to work on that Wednesday made for a short first week. He did not anticipate being on call at the emergency room over the coming weekend because Dr. Green, his replacement in the ER rotation, had worked the long Labor Day weekend shift just past. With his first weekend back presumably free, Dr. Hume hit the party scene. It was late Saturday night when the hospital called his house and requested his services at the emergency room. Myrt, who answered the phone, told the nurse who had placed the call that the doctor was not at home and she didn't know his whereabouts. Awhile later, the nurse called back with the same request; Myrt's response was the same. Still later the nurse called again, repeating the plea for Dr. Hume to come to the emergency room. This time Myrt told her that the doctor had returned home, but was drunk and in no condition to report to the hospital. With that, the calls ended.

The Suspension

By the middle of the following week, Dr. Hume received notice from the board president that his hospital privileges had been suspended. The stated rationale for the suspension was the missed call. Dr. Hume's suspension left only one remaining doctor available, insufficient coverage for the emergency room. A few days later, a hospital spokesman called *The Frontiersman* newspaper to announce that the emergency room was officially closed.

The newspaper ran a small article about the closure inside, but weighed in with a large front page editorial under the heading: Divorce Not An Answer. The editorial presented details of the suspension by way of personal metaphor; a love affair between the hospital association and Dr. Hume had somehow gone wrong and was ending in "divorce." The editorial lamented that someone always got hurt in a divorce, and in this case it was the community. Masterfully composed, it placed the readership as victims, or children, of the divorce. The editorial piece expressed wonder as to what could have warranted such action in the short period of time between the doctor's return from vacation and his suspension just a few days later. It trumpeted the doctor's skills, his philanthropic service, and the fact he had never been sued for malpractice. The article extended to the board a measure of understanding that its work was a time-consuming, unpaid service to the community, and even commended the board in that regard. But in a conspiratorial moment, the editorial expressed hope that the action did not result from the personalities of the hospital administration or board members. Finally, the piece called for the negotiation of differences between the parties involved and ended with another metaphor, suggesting that this was but one strike in a game that required three strikes before play ended.

The community had no way of knowing this was far from "strike one" in the long process that had ended with Dr. Hume's suspension. They could not have known the missed emergency room call was not the actual grounds for the suspension; in reality, the incident merely presented the opportunity for suspension. The board believed that full disclosure to the public could result in litigation for years to come. From the board's perspective, the suspension was a confidential personnel action that must remain private. They were not attempting to take his medical license, only to suspend his privileges to practice at the hospital. But this lack of communication from the board was perceived as arrogantly evasive. Townspeople were outraged that the beloved Dr. Hume had been suspended, and they wanted answers. Among those who insisted on an explanation was Mason LaZelle.

A Man in a Hurry

Born in Fairbanks, Alaska in August of 1918, LaZelle was a man of many missions. He was a tireless promoter and leader for community and economic development and all things Alaska. He had worked as a superintendent for the City of Anchorage and later as field engineer for Chugach Electric Association before coming to Palmer, where he worked for Matanuska Electric Association. After two years of service as a general foreman for MEA, LaZelle was named general manager of the electric utility. He was smart and aggressive, what they liked to call a "real go-getter." From his position as a general manager, he successfully championed the cause for bringing electricity to Alaska's remote Native villages. In his spare time, LaZelle pursued his great passion for flying. Even in his hobbies he was goal and achievement oriented, teaching ground school and rising to the rank of Major as a wing operations officer in the Civil Air Patrol. He volunteered time in a host of civic organizations, almost always in a leadership role, which was just the way he liked it. Mason LaZelle was used to being in charge and used to getting things done. He was politically astute, a skilled tactician, an effective public speaker, and a fine motivator of people in any organization he led. Like a good many men of power, he developed an ego to match his skills, but without question he could produce results. Personally many found LaZelle somewhat cool or standoffish, but to his close friends he was anything but that, showing a high level of thoughtfulness and intense loyalty. With this combination of professional and personal attributes, Mason LaZelle made for a bad enemy and a great friend, and Dr. Hume was one of his great friends.

Them and Us

On September 25, 1967, less than two weeks after Dr. Hume's suspension, a meeting was attended by nearly 100 members of the community to confer on the actions taken by the hospital board. The borough president conducted the proceedings at Swanson Elementary School. Practical questions voiced by the attendees included: How did the board plan to replace the surgical services they had recently suspended? How would the closure of the emergency room effect the community and the economic viability of the hospital? Why hadn't Dr. Hume's suspension been made public, and why wasn't there more public notice given for the ER closure? Clearly these were questions that ought to be posed to the hospital board. To begin a dialogue regarding these concerns, an ad hoc committee was established, with Mason LaZelle serving as chairman. That same night, LaZelle called the president of the hospital board, and requested a meeting between the ad hoc committee and the board. The board president said she would respond to the request the following afternoon. The next day, LaZelle received a call from the board president as promised. The president put LaZelle on notice that the call was being monitored, then reported she had decided against a meeting between the board and the ad hoc committee; instead she proposed a special meeting of the general membership of the hospital association. LaZelle pressed for a meeting between the committee and the board. Again he was told no, to which LaZelle asked if the decision not to meet was made by the whole board or solely by its president. The president responded that the bylaws gave her the authority to make the decision alone, without concurrence from the board. Mason LaZelle, as chairman, would have to report back, first to his committee and then to the interested members of the community, that the meeting they had envisioned would not be held. The ad hoc committee's meeting with the community was still seven days off, plenty of time for the chairman to study the hospital bylaws.

The whole business had the general population angered, perplexed, or both. Because the board was not talking—nor could it—those advocating the reinstatement of Dr. Hume's hospital privileges controlled much of the media and all of the word-of-mouth campaign, a sizable information source in a small town. The newspaper printed a number of letters in support of the doctor. Some writers justified the missed emergency room call, while others directly condemned the board's lack of foresight in its actions. Mason LaZelle contributed letters to the editor and also penned a paid piece to keep the community apprised of the situation and how it was being handled. His formidable communication skills extended to the written word. All the board submitted for publication was an excerpt from the *American Hospital Association Journal*. The article spoke, in part, to the responsibilities of a doctor practicing at a hospital and the responsibility of a governing board to maintain legal and moral standards at a hospital. The article was square on topic, but probably few readers possessed enough knowledge of the local situation to read between the lines and understand the submission's full intended message.

Most of the tactics employed by the groups on either side of the suspension issue were apparent. The LaZelle group attempted to expand and slightly blur the issues so the board would eventually *have* to respond. Yet any response would open a Pandora's box to specific questions regarding Dr. Hume, questions the board could not legally answer. LaZelle still wanted a private meeting between his ad hoc group and the board, but the prospect of any such closed-door meeting with Mason LaZelle, one in which he might gain control, held little allure for the board. The hospital board held out for a special meeting over which the board would preside and would have a greater hand in controlling. These were legal and largely open tactics employed by both groups, but a few in the community felt less bound by the restrictions of the law or even fair play. For a very small fringe element not associated with the high profile groups, the end justified the means, even when those means were terrorist in nature. In the small community, the board members completely lacked anonymity and were easy targets of crank phone calls and nighttime gunshots in close proximity to their homes. One board member received a late night phone message from a caller with a menacing voice warning that a cross would soon be burned on the board member's lawn. They received threats to their homes and livelihoods. Some board members had the uneasy feeling their phones were tapped. Not all of the board members took the threats seriously, reasoning that it was all just a lot of loose talk, no doubt fueled by liquid courage. But some board members did take the words seriously and felt fearful. None believed Dr. Hume would have condoned any such activity.

Mason LaZelle's review of the hospital bylaws was the main subject of the October 2nd community meeting. LaZelle made a case for a number of bylaw changes and additions. He expressed a need to tighten up bylaw language, establish provisions for increased public involvement, and allow for the orderly removal of board members. Those in attendance agreed with the suggested bylaw modifications and were quickly provided petitions to sign to get the changes placed before the general membership of the hospital association at a yet unscheduled special meeting. The ad hoc committee was asked by the attendees to renew its attempt to meet with the board prior to the special meeting. The committee, meeting the following day, drafted a letter to the board president officially repeating its request for a meeting. The request was finally granted, and the ad hoc committee was scheduled to meet with the board on October 19, 1967, during a regular board session.

The Battle Cry

Armed to the teeth with questions for the board, proposed bylaw changes, and with a sympathetic crowd of onlookers behind him, Mason LaZelle confronted the board about its recent actions. He even had an anecdotal story to tell. The story had appeared in the local paper a week earlier, and it seemed the perfect example of just one of the serious ramifications of the board's flawed action in suspending the hospital surgeon. A local high school teacher in extreme pain had been transported by pickup to the office of Dr. Hume. The man was too ill to walk downstairs for an examination, so Dr. Hume journeyed outside to the truck to see him. In short order, Dr. Hume diagnosed the ailment as an appendicitis. Because the doctor was not allowed to work at the hospital, and the emergency room was closed, the man was rushed to Anchorage, sixty miles away, for an operation. But, LaZelle went on, the man didn't make it to the hospital in time and his appendix ruptured. Although the man did survive his ordeal, the story remained proof positive of what could go wrong without a staff surgeon and an available emergency room.

Though empathetic of the situation, the board was not swayed. Even with all the pointed questions and talk of petitions, the board members didn't budge. The audience, with unrealistic expectations of the meeting, grew frustrated with the board's failure to provide definitive answers to questions, its reluctance to co-operate, and its defensive posture. Some of those in attendance believed a resolution could have been reached, but in viewing the proceedings it became apparent the board had its mind made up. Then it got ugly. Frustration boiled over into anger. In answering a question about the economic viability of a hospital without the services of its only surgeon, the board president carefully explained that financial considerations did not override the legal, moral, or ethical aspects of running a hospital. To many community members, this didn't sound as much like an explanation as it did a character attack on the doctor they loved. The tenor of the meeting began to change to one of general unruliness. People, sensing the implication of the president's statement, began to shout slogans such as, "I'd rather have Doc Hume operate on me drunk, than any other doctor sober," and that became the battle cry for many of them. Facing the onslaught of the now-overheated session, coupled with the personal threats they had been enduring, some of the board members began to waver in their convictions, but somehow despite the intense pressure, they were able to make it through the meeting with their ranks intact. There was more conflict to come.

The Last Showdown

The special membership meeting was scheduled for November 3rd. Between the confrontational board meeting and the special membership meeting, the hospital board sent the newspaper a clarification of the first aid services available at the hospital in lieu of the past emergency room services. That was not the only undertaking; they were actively gathering proxies. It was no secret; Mason LaZelle knew about it and complained of the board's efforts in a paid piece run in the newspaper the day before the special meeting. A realist, LaZelle probably already knew he had been bested. The meeting convened on a Friday evening in the Swanson School multipurpose room and all the players were there: the board, the ad hoc committee, and the members of the Valley Hospital Association—approximately 200 people packed into the small pastel-paneled room. Up for consideration were ten bylaw revisions. The membership would be voting on the rights for citizens to be heard during board meetings, a procedure for the removal of directors, the reduction of board members from eleven to seven, and a provision that would allow for board meetings to be called without the concurrence of the president. Early in the meeting, a motion was voted on that would have disallowed the use of board-solicited proxies in the bylaw balloting. Of course all proxies were allowed for *that* vote, and the motion failed by a count of 304 to 105. It was unclear if the motion had been proposed in the faint hope of actually limiting the use of the proxies, or to ascertain early the strength of the board's support. In any case, the results were crystal clear; it was going to be an early and unhappy night for Hume supporters. Getting down to the business of the bylaws, a motion was made and seconded that all ten proposed bylaw changes not be adopted and that the board be commended for its hard work. That the board be commended for its hard work? That, in the face of defeat was painful. Before barely a protest could be uttered or discussions ensue, there was a call for the question. A hasty motion was made to table the action and stave off a vote altogether, but it failed. Finally, they all voted on the proposed bylaws. With a final tally of 291 to 115, the changes failed in their entirety. It was all over but the shouting, and indeed there were shouts, "I'd rather have Doc Hume operate on me drunk, than any other doctor sober!"

How could it have happened? How could it have all ended in such a swift and crushing defeat? It was a humiliating loss for LaZelle and the pro-Hume group but perhaps not as surprising as was initially thought. As loved as he was, by the fall of 1967, Dr. Hume did have his detractors. He had touched a great many lives in a positive manner in the small community, but through his heavy drinking, he had touched many in negative ways too. Of all the excessive drinking that occurred in the still largely frontier town, his seemed the least compatible with his occupation. But that is an incomplete answer to the question of the bylaw defeat. Some of the cause must be placed on the strategy and tactics of Mason LaZelle. LaZelle believed the board had taken an action that was harmful to the community at large and specifically to his good friend Dr. Hume. There is no question that he was passionate in righting what he perceived was a wrong, through legal means. Once he made up his mind, he was a bulldog on an issue, and that was part of the problem. LaZelle moved fast on an issue that required patience, for the public generally assimilates information slowly and, when pushed, a public in doubt tends to vote no. For many, the new bylaw language appeared heavy-handed and nothing short of a hostile takeover of the board, a board made up of friends and neighbors.

In the Line of Fire

Dr. Hume never spoke or appeared at any public forum assembled to endorse his reinstatement at the hospital. He carried on his private practice, which was thriving, but at risk. People needed a doctor who could see them at the hospital. When a new doctor inevitably arrived in Palmer and the emergency room reopened, Dr. Hume knew his practice would suffer. But for the present, business was good and many of his office patients, before their examinations, expressed indignation at his suspension and pledged their allegiance to him and his practice. He accepted those offerings gratefully but quickly changed the subject to the reason for the office visit. In a few special circumstances he made a personal effort to inform his patients of the suspension. One of these situations involved a woman near the end of her pregnancy who had a history of difficulties in labor. Dr. Hume visited her and her husband at home and related in a matter-of-fact tone that although the couple probably already heard, he wanted to tell them personally that he was no longer able to practice at the hospital and therefore they should make other arrangements. He did not let on one way or another whether he thought the suspension was justified; neither did he let show a hint of bitterness. That visit meant a lot to the couple, for Dr. Hume's concern for the woman and her baby had superseded any of his own personal feelings of anger, hurt, or shame over the suspension.

Although he successfully kept his emotions masked in a professional setting, he had a hard time keeping them in check elsewhere. All kinds of feelings came to the surface when he was drinking, but when they poured out of him all at once, the only identifiable emotion was anger. The sarcastic comments that once marked his nastiest moments elevated to vile caustic remarks. Where people had once gathered around him in the local bars, now many avoided him; some even got up and left their tables upon his entry rather than be the victim of his sharp tongue. At home it was the same old story—he just wasn't around much. And so the nighttime cycle continued for the family that waited at home. Initially they eagerly anticipated his arrival, but as the hours passed, eagerness turned to dread with the uncertainty of his level of inebriation and the darkness of his mood. His temper had gotten worse after the opportunities of overturning the suspension had been exhausted. When he was at home he seemed more agitated and was hypersensitive to any perceived slight. In the face of all that had happened professionally and personally, he expected complete unwavering loyalty from his family, the kind of loyalty that did not allow criticism of any kind. You were either for him or against him; it was that simple. One night, he came home drunk and found Myrt in the bathroom toweling off toddler John after his bath. He came into the bathroom and began groping Myrt as she dried their son. Having enough, Myrt spoke sharply and told her husband to get his drunken hands off her. He exploded with rage. If you weren't for him, you were against him. Pulling her from the bathroom, he beat her savagely. The kids screamed in terror, "Daddy stop it, stop it!" but his ferocity kept everyone at bay until the outburst played itself out.

Recovery for many alcoholics comes only after reaching their personal rock bottom. Beating one's wife in front of the children would certainly fit most alcoholics' definition of rock bottom. It did for Dr. Hume. At long last he seemed to come to his senses. He stayed home, and although he plainly was bored, he made a real effort at breaking free from drink and the way of life that went with it. He put together jigsaw puzzles and worked crosswords. He played games with Myrt. He was trying to reclaim what he had damaged and what he had almost lost. Dr. Hume had reason for hope on the home front and reason for hope professionally too, for Mason LaZelle was back on the case, and he had a new plan.

Down but Never Out

LaZelle had been defeated, but not broken. There wasn't a lot of quit in Mason LaZelle. The lost bylaw vote was a step back but only that—a mere miscalculation. There were other ways to get things done, and LaZelle had one figured. If he couldn't bring about change and get his friend reinstated from the outside, he would do it from the inside. The February hospital board elections were just around the corner, and LaZelle was going to be a candidate.

13

A Great Brother

The All-American Boy

Dr. Hume's eldest son, Frank, was a low key, easygoing, average boy in a house full of beautiful, smart, extroverted women. It didn't bother him a bit. He admired his sisters but did not envy them. They did their thing and he did his. He was much too happy and busy in his own pursuits to waste time on envy. He was the one in the family who was most secure with being by himself. He was not a loner, but Frank didn't care for the spotlight as much as the others, content instead to blend into the crowd. In social interaction, he was most comfortable in one-on-one situations or in small groups, where he was talkative and outgoing. Though he was an above average student, other interests competed for his time. For him, the biggest drawback of school was that it took place indoors, with lessons based on the discoveries of others. Frank wanted to explore and discover for himself. His classroom of choice was the great outdoors. For all their differences, Frank's siblings admired him too. They admired his independent ways and his hands-on approach to life. When they were with Frank they had fun, but they were also safe. He was not impulsive and he was not a risk taker. Frank was not altogether passive—he possessed a bit of a temper—but he was generally kind and gentle. His sisters could tell that their brother would be a good man. His parents knew this too.

Myrt was close to all six children, believing they were her life's calling, and Frank was no exception. She adored her eldest son. The doctor, whose interaction with his children was at best pedestrian, had a bond with Frank that grew through the years. In some ways Dr. Hume probably even admired Frank, for Frank displayed qualities of the young Vinnie that had long ago been conceded to adult life and the overwhelming pressures

and responsibilities of the medical profession. Like Frank, young Vinnie had been independent and freewheeling, taking life on his own terms. Bright enough to perform to high standards in school, but too fun-loving to take school very seriously. Dr. Hume's obvious family favorite was daughter Cindy, but even that preference tended to enhance Frank's stature,

Frank and Cindy. (*Hume family collection*)

for the tight association between Cindy and Frank must have reminded Dr. Hume of his relationship with his sister Doreen.

They Seemed Like Twins

The relationship between Frank and Cindy was deep and multifaceted. In addition to being brother and sister, they were also close friends and playmates. As the elder of the two, Frank often served as Cindy's mentor. Once when she was quite young, Cindy, in possession of $9.95, wanted a nickel in the worst way so she could say she had "ten whole dollars." Thinking of no other way to quickly obtain the money, she dipped into her mother's change purse. Frank caught her in the act. He told her she was stealing and said that if she wanted the money all she had to do was ask and their mom would have given it to her. The talk made an impression, and Cindy never stole anything again.

Frank and Cindy had many fun—even crazy—adventures. In early grade school, Frank and Cindy, along with childhood friend Karl Kopperud, once successfully crawled through every culvert they encountered on their walk home from school. Frank thought of a lot of outdoorsy things to do. For instance, in the "big woods," the heavily forested area to the west of the

Hume's log home, Frank and Cindy ran a trap line. The big woods was also home to a tree fort constructed by Frank and some of his friends. Cindy had full access to the fort; that is, until one fateful day when Cindy showed up and found a "no girls allowed" sign attached to the structure. She was devastated by this betrayal. Sure, she was a girl, but wasn't she one of the boys too? She felt so badly, she couldn't even eat. Finally after a few days, Frank came to her and, gesturing for her to follow, said, "Come on." He led her into the big woods to the site of the "boys only" tree fort, and showed her that he had begun construction of a "girls only" fort.

In winter, they sometimes harnessed the family's huge black Labrador, Sam, to a sled. Frank ran beside Sam while the dog pulled Cindy and Starr in the sled. Frank and Cindy also spent a lot of time together at the lake property, boating, fishing, and hunting ducks. Sometimes the doctor would join them. Generally Cindy was stuck cleaning their catch, but she thought it was a small price to pay for being allowed to go along. On occasion, Frank and Cindy went by boat up a stream that fed into Finger Lake and floated back down, splashing and making all kinds of commotion on their way in an attempt at "fish herding." They then moved ahead to their favorite fishing hole where the fish had presumably schooled. Those summer days on the lake were pure adventure for Frank and Cindy, like something right out of the pages of *Huckleberry Finn*. Who could know what adventure lay just around the bend.

With His Friends

Frank was a well-liked boy with a wide array of friends. Beyond sharing his love for the outdoors, Frank's buddies were a varied bunch. Certainly there was no pigeonholing Frank's personality by observing his assortment of friends. Two of his closest friends were Chris Downs and Raymond Fuller. Both boys seemed like opposites in contrast to Frank's personality. Chris was the toughest of his friends, willing to physically challenge anyone he believed had done him or a friend wrong. Raymond was not physically aggressive, but had the handsome look of a bad boy that, coupled with a bit of youthful brashness and a gift for playing a rocking guitar, made Raymond Fuller very popular with the girls. It never hurt to have a tough guy for a friend or a guy around who was good at pulling in the girls. Both were admirable traits, and Frank held both Chris and Raymond in high regard.

Frank and his buddies invested themselves completely in all-boy type hobbies and adventures which they sometimes referred to as "safaris." Frank liked to tear into small engines that wouldn't run. If he and the guys couldn't repair them, at least they could learn how they worked. They were big on building things, digging tunnels, and cutting trails. They all admired guns and knives. One of their safaris included the pursuit of ducks on Finger Lake. Frank, along with pal Max Medima, set out on a path of duck destruction, envisioning a bountiful harvest and much fine dining. They verbally pumped each other up with, "We'll pound those ducks with bullets." But like all young and inexperienced predators, the two boys expended a lot of effort with no net result; the ducks lived to fly another day. On another occasion, the same two ventured out to Mud Lake in search of ducks. They found no waterfowl, but they did bag a large hornets' nest with a 20 gauge shotgun, forcing them to beat a hasty retreat in the face of an angry swarm of hornets.

Frank with pal Chris Downs. (*Hume family collection*)

Teens enjoyed a lot of unsupervised recreational shooting in those days, and Frank's circle experienced their share of the resulting mishaps. One day, Frank and his friends were hunting for ptarmigan when a .22 caliber collapsible survival rifle, commonly carried in private aircraft, went off, sending a bullet near another boy's head. On another outing, an angry man told the boys to be more careful with their shooting because bullets had come dangerously close to his home. The boys did not realize the distance capabilities of their firearms. On yet another occasion, Chris Downs was superficially wounded by a .22 bullet that had ricocheted. Such instances served as short-term wake-up calls for gun safety but, as is human nature, as time passed so did some of the awareness to the inherent danger of the weapons.

The best part of the boys' safaris was the freedom involved. No adult supervision was the first ingredient to having a truly good time. One favorite outing was undertaken by Frank, Kerry Williams, and Frank's cousin, David Starkey, Doreen's son who visited for the 1967 summer. A bush pilot owed Dr. Hume for medical services but couldn't pay. The doctor suggested a trade—a fly-in fishing trip, not for himself but for Frank and his friends. The deal was struck. Soon the three boys were winging their way into a remote area to be dropped off on a sandbar for the fantastic experience of fishing an Alaska salmon run all by themselves.

One of the safaris could have ended unhappily. Frank and another boy set about on an overnight canoe trip. Dr. Hume was scheduled to pick them up at the end of the journey. Before leaving home, the other boy's mother made a passing remark about the doctor's alcoholism, which stuck with the boy. During the course of the trip, bursting with inquisitiveness, the boy finally asked Frank the direct,

The mighty fishermen after cleaning and filleting their catch. From left: Frank Hume, cousin David Starkey, and Kerry Williams. (*Hume family collection*)

if rather blunt, question he had on his mind, "So, what's it like having an alcoholic for a parent?" Frank bristled and snapped back, "There's nothing wrong with my dad. He's a perfectly good dad!" The boy instantly realized he had made a serious misstep with his question, knowing it could put an end to all the fun. But much to his relief, that's where the matter ended and he was grateful to Frank for not carrying a grudge. The two had a great time for the rest of the trip, and a sober Dr. Hume was waiting for them as planned when they put into shore.

Coming Into His Own

By Frank's freshman year at Palmer High School, he had already entered into young adulthood. He was still mostly a conformist and displayed excellent deportment, but he was beginning to have his own opinions. His appearance was changing too. He had always been well dressed, attired in pinstriped or plaid men's button-down dress shirts, but his sandy hair was a little longer now, in the style of the times, and he made more of an effort to comb it. His voice had deepened. His face had an angular shape, his features slightly exaggerated with a wide nose and a wide mouth that produced about the biggest smile around. Important changes developed in his personal relationships as well.

Frank's relationship with his father had evolved into one of more equal standing. They even journeyed on a couple of fly-in hunting trips together. The elder Hume's drinking still got in the way, but in strange fashion it sometimes seemed to shape the relationship, at least in the short-term, in a positive way. The doctor, returning home in his cups, passed by Frank's room on the way to his and Myrt's. Sometimes he stopped at Frank's room, even waking him, to tell him of his nighttime escapades or of the people and conversations. Perhaps it wasn't much, but it was sharing, and from the doctor that was to be prized on any level. If the change in the relationship between Dr. Hume and Frank could be typified by a specific event, it was their fishing trip to Talkeetna. The road system had finally linked the small town with the rest of south-central Alaska. One afternoon, the doctor drove himself and Frank to Talkeetna to catch some fish. During the course of the outing the doctor started drinking, drinking so much he couldn't drive home. Frank, though several years underage, got behind the wheel, and with his father sound asleep beside him, drove back home. The doctor was proud of Frank for that. After all those years as a care receiver, the boy had reversed the roles and had taken care of his dad. It was a symbolic passing of the torch.

Frank's personal relationships with girls were changing too. There was one girl in particular he had always liked. In the sixth grade, he had been Kathy Kincaid's first boyfriend and had even given her a ring as a token of his affection; a simple metal band with a flat spot on top. By the fall of 1967, he began to view Kathy with renewed interest. At a huge bonfire near the train depot, an annual event kicking off the high school sports season, Frank wheeled up to Kathy on his motorcycle. The two of them kidded around a bit and flirted. Finally Frank leaned forward and kissed her. It was her first kiss, a meaningful moment as all first kisses are, lingering in her memory. To summon up the courage for a kiss, and to have it reciprocated was tremendously exhilarating for Frank as well.

For many teens growing up in small towns, life is an endless struggle to "get hip." During the uprising of the youth movement in the 1960s, getting hip was of supreme importance to young people across the nation. The desire was no different for teens living in frontier Alaska, but the challenges of achieving it were greater. At least they had the music—all those great tunes that were the hallmark of hipness. Listening was one thing, but playing those tunes in a band was the ultimate in cool. Raymond Fuller played in a band, and although he and Frank had an on-again-off-again relationship typical of youthful friendships, their bond rekindled when Frank expressed an interest in learning to play the guitar.

The Accident

It was the afternoon of Saturday, February 3, 1968. Dr. Hume, still abstaining from alcohol, and Myrt were amusing themselves by working on a jigsaw puzzle, when they took note of the time. It was getting late, and Frank had not returned from checking his trap line along the Matanuska River. Making his rounds, Frank was riding a snowmachine the family had recently acquired. Concerned, Myrt drove downtown to the drugstore to check if anyone had seen her son. While there, she received a call from the doctor. He told her to come home—Frank had just phoned from the Fuller's home where he had stopped to visit Raymond.

After visiting awhile, Frank was preparing to leave for home when Raymond asked him to wait just a minute while he unloaded his .22 caliber rifle, a Remington Model 572 pump, which had been inadvertently placed in a gun cabinet while still loaded. Raymond knew that loaded guns in the Fuller home were against the rules, and so he set about unloading the pump, holding in the little button and working the slide. He successfully ejected two live rounds, but somehow the third was discharged directly into Frank's chest. Frank bent over and said, "You shot me." Raymond dropped the gun and embraced Frank, helping him to a nearby bedroom where he laid Frank down. Then Raymond ran to the telephone and summoned help. Alaska State Trooper Fillingim responded to the scene and was met by Raymond, who took him to where he had placed Frank just inside the doorway of the bedroom. The trooper could detect no pulse or breathing in the fallen boy. Dr. Cunningham was contacted and, upon examination, declared Frank Hume dead at 5:30 P.M.

Meanwhile, the Humes were wondering why Frank hadn't returned. They phoned the Fuller home and spoke with Raymond's grandmother, who lived in the home's basement apartment. She seemed confused and provided no answers about Frank's whereabouts. Myrt had a bad feeling, suspecting that Frank had been in a snowmachine accident. She put on her coat and headed for the front door. Opening it, she found Dr. Cunningham, about to knock. Speaking from the landing, Dr. Cunningham gave them all the terrible news. As kindly as it was offered, no one was equipped for receiving this kind of information. The impact of the words instantly scrambled and overloaded the family's emotions. Pain seized them before they could even begin to comprehend what they had learned. Dr. Hume looked as if he had been hit in the stomach. Both parents appeared to disintegrate under the force and gravity of this incomprehensible situation. In mindless, thoughtless agony, Dr. Hume lashed out verbally at those around him, inflicting still more damage on his suffering family.

The Funeral

The pathologist's report confirmed what had been suspected; Frank had died of internal bleeding. The .22 caliber bullet had entered his left upper chest and severed his aorta. The investigation consisted of several short interviews which gave no indication that a criminal act had taken place. The incident was ruled an accident.

Despite their unimaginable grief, the Humes had much to do, as the funeral was to be conducted just three days after the accident. They had to notify out-of-state family and friends of Frank's death, prepare for visitors and overnight house guests, and plan the funeral service. During all of this, a salesman dropped by the Hume home in an attempt to sell them a kind of hood that would fit over their son's coffin at burial. The peddler explained that without the hood, the weight of the backfill could collapse the coffin in on Frank for all eternity. The conjuring up of such a horrendous mental picture for the sake of making a sale drew the wrath of the doctor. Literally throwing the salesman out of the house and down the stairs, he yelled after him, "You are nothing but a ghoul!" before slamming the door.

The small community, so recently torn apart when forced to take sides over the doctor's hospital suspension, rallied once more in a show of support for the Humes at the funeral service for Frank. The service was conducted on the afternoon of Tuesday, February 6, 1968, in the beautiful log United Protestant Church, with the Reverend William Miller officiating. Many of those in attendance were Frank's friends and classmates. For nearly all of them, this was their first confrontation with the finality of death. Most had never been to a funeral, and some of them had never been inside a church before that day. The whole experience was overwhelming, especially for Raymond Fuller, who had somehow summoned the courage to attend. He sat in the back of the church, his knees drawn up to his body, his head buried in his knees. No one begrudged his attendance. The church did not have enough seating for the large number of people who attended. Many stood, and some were forced to stand outside. The service was very hard on everyone; open crying was heard throughout the ceremony. In addition to the loss they all felt, their hearts were torn by the effect the service had on the Hume family, particularly the doctor. Dr. Hume's grief was completely uncontrolled, reducing him to deep sobs. He was inconsolable. At the close of the service, the crowd filed by the open casket saying final goodbyes to Frank Hume. Then the pallbearers, made up from a group of Frank's young friends, removed the casket.

Grief is not a tidy emotion that can be contained within a funeral service. The service was only the first step in the healing process. The three eldest Hume girls, April, Dawn, and Cindy reached out to Raymond Fuller in an attempt to help him with his pain.

Myrt's recovery process was greatly aided by the care of Reverend Miller, who came to sit with her every day for the next three weeks. Myrt had a long journey ahead in her grief, but at least she was getting started. Dr. Hume refused to meet the reverend or accept any kind of assistance from anyone in the matter of his son's death; instead he isolated himself emotionally and sank ever lower into a sorrow that showed no limit.

14

Blue Days, Black Nights

On Point

Most people who knew the all-business Mason LaZelle only in passing couldn't have imagined him capable of writing a letter of condolence that expressed humility, caring, and tenderness, but that is exactly what he did. Following Frank's death, LaZelle wrote a letter to the doctor and Myrt. The letter conveyed sympathy, respect, and encouragement in working through theirs and their children's grief. It offered encouragement on other fronts as well. LaZelle wrote indirectly about the doctor's use of alcohol, referring to it as his "problem." He said people were heartened by his efforts to solve that problem, alluding to the doctor's preceding period of abstinence. He encouraged the doctor not to relax those efforts, because so many were depending on him. He suggested that a healthy distraction from the grief was in order. Such a distraction, a useful one, was working to resolve the troubles with the hospital. In this area LaZelle expressed the need for patience and long-term resolve.

LaZelle had himself received a lesson in patience from his dealings with the hospital board just a few months earlier, and he was not one to make the same mistake twice.

The start of the February 15, 1968, annual meeting of the Valley Hospital Association was delayed by a throng of citizens wishing to join the association and by those registering proxies. The membership swelled from the previous year's total of 383 to a record 789. At stake was the election of four board members. Three current board members, whose terms were expiring, were vying for reelection, including the board president.

When the votes were counted, not one of them was reelected; four new citizens took their places. Among them was Mason LaZelle. Now it seemed only a matter of time before Dr. Hume would regain his privileges to practice at the hospital.

Twelve days after his election to the hospital board, Mason LaZelle took the pilot's seat of Matanuska Electric Association's white and red Cessna 185 for a work-related trip to Nulato and Unalakleet. Accompanying him were two MEA employees, Phil McRae and Alex Fuller, father of Raymond Fuller. Prior to their 8:58 A.M. departure from Palmer, LaZelle was briefed in person by flight service personnel about the marginal weather conditions in his flight path. As an experienced and accomplished pilot, LaZelle was confident he could make the trip safely. At about 10:00 A.M. a Yentna River trapper saw the MEA Cessna in flight and on course. After that sighting, the plane and the men disappeared.

The disappearance touched off a vast search for the men. Dozens of pilots and observers took to the air, logging thousands of hours, often in marginal flying conditions. The potential loss of three respected family men was devastating to the small community. They had to be found. No one could bear the thought that they were out in the winter wilderness somewhere, alive and suffering. Reports came in of weak distress calls, rifle signals, sightings of flares, and markings in the snow. None of the leads proved fruitful except for the temporary hope they provided. Townspeople generously donated time and money to the search. Women, including Myrt, cooked for the searchers, delivering meals to the weary pilots and observers. The Matanuska Valley Lions Club and several other organizations got involved. But try as everyone did, there was no sign of the men. As hope faded for a rescue, fewer search flights were taken. Eventually the searching stopped—it would resume in the summer, after most of the mountain snow had melted. The searchers hoped then they could find the wreckage and recover the bodies.

Beware of Darkness

Emotions were running high in Palmer. Dr. Hume's hospital suspension and the split in the community were still fresh, as was the now-failed attempt at taking over the board. Frank's death had been a tremendous blow, and now the disappearance of the three men left the community reeling. Everyone seemed to have been touched directly or indirectly by the tragedies. Rumors and conspiracy theories abounded on the devil's radio. One outrageous theory suggested that the anti-Hume fringe had somehow sabotaged the MEA Cessna in an effort to keep LaZelle from seizing control of the board and getting the doctor reinstated. The doctor had a theory of his own in regard to Frank's death. The notion came alive when he was drinking, and he was drinking now like never before. He had a completely unsupported belief that there was more to the shooting than was being told, and that it wasn't an accident. His beliefs probably were based on a personal sense of helplessness to which he was not accustomed. He advanced the theory to his family members who disagreed with his speculations, which he took as an affront. You were either for him or against him. He was angry and growing angrier. Out on the town, he seemed to be constantly looking for a fight—a fight or a game.

He was completely stripped of inhibitions now. The liquor and pills exacerbated his inappropriate behavior. His lack of restraint was often exhibited in gambling. He shot pool with players who were more skillful and less inebriated. To help combat his opponents' sobriety, he began carrying a small oxygen cylinder in his car trunk and would excuse himself to breathe from it between games. He insisted on playing double-or-nothing, which escalated the stakes rapidly. One night he lost $3,500 to a close friend. The next day when he told Myrt of his loss, she called the bank to stop payment. His friend tried to cash the check, only to find it was no good. He called the Hume home for an explanation. Myrt answered and gave the man a piece of her mind, telling him that he should be ashamed of himself for taking advantage of a drunk. That, of course, was not the end of the matter. Dr. Hume knew he couldn't get future games if he didn't pay his gambling debts, so he borrowed the sum from Neal Wright. His high-stakes games continued, some reaching as high as $5,000. Bar patrons were used to games of chance, but not with stakes so high, and they all gathered around to watch.

Dr. Hume played pool with one person more than any others, a young man in his early twenties—a man who generally beat him. One night the younger player was way ahead in the winnings and began to feel guilty about taking so much money from the doctor. The young man saw an opportunity to let Dr. Hume win without making his mercy obvious, which would have only served to humiliate the doctor further by making it appear as if he were a charity case. There were no balls left on the table as the doctor's competitor lined up his shot. He knew he had to make the shot look good, so he planned to just touch the eight ball and not to sink it, leaving the doctor a straight easy shot and the win. But he miscalculated and sank the eight ball cleanly. A great whoop went up from the audience, an audience which had never witnessed such a close, high-stakes game. Amidst the cheers and congratulations, the winner cast a glance at Dr. Hume, who seemed to virtually implode, crushed by the loss and alone in his defeat.

Despite his nocturnal misadventures, the doctor continued to report for work each day at the basement office. Elayne Williams was still there, and so was Arleta O'Connor, who had joined the staff as an aide. Mrs. O'Connor's brother was a hospital board member during the time of Dr. Hume's suspension, which could have given rise to a hostile work environment, but to his credit, Dr. Hume never made mention of her brother's involvement in the loss of his hospital privileges. The office was still doing a very good business, but for some it was troubling to see the doctor. He could aid them just as before, but his patients couldn't help him, and he was probably the one most in need.

A few friends reached out to him. Neal tried to help too, but even he was unnerved by the doctor's depth of depression and his appetite for self-destruction. Neighbors from the lake thought taking the doctor on an out-of-town fishing trip to Talkeetna might prove restful. But on the way there, he began talking about Frank, which in a short time reduced him to sobs. Through his tears, he repeated, "He was such a good boy." Upon reaching their destination, the others went fishing as planned, and Dr. Hume headed for the bar. He was making little progress in dealing with his grief.

Riding Out the Storm
Every family and individual works through grief differently.

For the Hume children, the mourning was further complicated by a parent in the throes of addiction, whose behavior was becoming scarier. For awhile, the forward momentum of their high-achieving ways carried them through, but that could only last so long. The kids needed an emotional rest from the chaos, stress, and all the crying.

Myrt needed a reprieve, too. She couldn't give up or give in to depression, as she still had five children to raise. But it was a strain, and there wasn't much to be hopeful about. For her, the future amounted to getting through one day to reach the next. Her only positive diversion was her sewing machine, which allowed her to immerse herself in a myriad of projects that gave her respite from her troubles. Her only other avenue of peace was prayer, which as a woman of faith, she undertook in earnest.

The girls had a plan to help distract their mother. They strongly urged her to enter the Mrs. Matanuska Valley contest. Entrants were judged on homemaking abilities, poise, personality, character, and grooming. Mom had all that going for her and more, the girls thought, so with their urging she entered. The contest got off to a bit of a rocky start when, during the contestant interviews, Myrt was asked if she was willing to travel if she were chosen as Mrs. Matanuska Valley. Myrt answered no to the question, elaborating that her family needed her at home. Later in the day, Myrt was modeling a short formal dress that she and April had designed and she had sewn, when she overheard a judge remark that the dress looked store-bought. Myrt took exception to the statement, and in her customary directness pointed out to the judge that the dress was in fact an original of her own making. Myrt did well in the remaining competitive events, including entertaining a five-year-old child, flower arranging (using plastic flowers) and preparing a seafood dish. Though Myrt did not win, she was awarded the first runner-up prize for her efforts.

The contest was an all-too-brief break from the turmoil. The doctor's drinking and doping was so out of control that Myrt would have rathered he be out with another woman than out drinking. She would willingly make that tradeoff for sobriety. As it was, she and the kids were sometimes forced into hiding to escape her husband's unpredictable periods of wrath. They escaped to their motel or lake house. Sometimes they drove to Anchorage and sat through drive-in movies just to evade the doctor.

There seemed to be an endless supply of emotional blows to endure. Frank had not been buried in February, as the ground was still frozen. With the arrival of spring, Myrt asked the funeral home about scheduling a graveside service and burial, thinking this might finally bring some closure to the grieving process. She learned that Frank had already been buried, without notice to the family.

Shortly after, the doctor and Myrt went fishing on Finger Lake. In a lucid conversation, the doctor admitted he needed to make some changes in his personal life. To that end, he suggested the likelihood for success might be greater if Myrt and the kids lived elsewhere for awhile. He said he needed time to straighten himself out. Myrt and kids packed up and left for the summer to visit relatives in Texas.

As spring gave way to summer, the search for the missing MEA flight resumed. Finally, on July 24, 1968, five months after the plane disappeared, an Anchorage pilot spotted what looked to be the wreckage of the MEA plane. Several days later, the weather permitted a U.S. Army helicopter to touch down at the crash site, where positive identification of the plane and its occupants was made. The bodies were recovered a short time later. A subsequent investigation of the accident by the National Transportation Safety Board concluded that the pilot had attempted aircraft operation beyond his experience and/or ability. The Cessna probably experienced icing that resulted in air foil distortion, which caused the plane to drop rapidly and strike the side of a mountain. It had all happened very quickly. Thankfully, the three men had not suffered. Funeral services were conducted in Palmer for Phil McRae, age 37, on August 1st, and a day later, for Alex Fuller, age 46. Services for Mason LaZelle were held in Anchorage on August 3rd, the day before what would have been his fiftieth birthday. Dr. Hume was named as an honorary pallbearer.

Dr. Hume wanted to keep his promise to Myrt. He went to Seattle for a course in the care of heart and stroke patients conducted at the University of Washington. While there, he stayed at the home of a friend where he made serious inroads into getting off the pills he had been taking. His heavy drinking, however, continued unabated.

After his return to Alaska, he and Myrt agreed that she and the kids, back only a short time from Texas, should prepare to leave Palmer for good. Years earlier they had purchased a farm near Corvallis, Oregon as an investment. The doctor would join the family at a later date.

The night before his family was to depart, the doctor went downtown to make the rounds of the local bars. In one of the establishments, he unleashed a torrent of verbal abuse on a stranger—a stranger who wasn't aware he was a doctor, and who didn't know he had met with so much recent sorrow. The only thing the stranger knew was that a drunk was mouthing off. A fight ensued and the doctor was savagely beaten. The next morning, he helped load his family's luggage into Preston and Millie Williams's car for transport to the airport. It was painfully obvious that he had been in a fight, but not a word was said about it. He accompanied his family to the airport in Anchorage, but instead of seeing them off at their boarding gate, he headed to the lounge.

Without Limits

The Corvallis farm's livable dwellings were all occupied as rentals, which forced Myrt and the kids into lodging at a nearby motel. They lived that way for several weeks before Myrt ordered a three-bedroom, doublewide mobile home, which was placed on the farm. The trailer was a step down compared to their home in Palmer, which the kids had not wanted to leave in the first place. To them, the general atmosphere of Corvallis seemed cold and unfriendly. They missed the people of Palmer.

Now that Dr. Hume was on his own, any remaining inhibitions, restrictions, or even obligations were gone. The pills he had discarded in Seattle were replaced with injections of morphine in Palmer. In the course of the workday, he would sometimes slip out for a quick drink during lunchtime. His habit of nightly barhopping was beginning to wear thin with some of the locals, particularly the tavern owners. Simply put, Dr. Hume was bad for business. He could clear a place out in short order with his inappropriate and mean remarks. Some of the comments were based on his knowledge of the confidential matters of his profession. He said a lot of things for shock value. In one establishment, he berated the bartender, a long time friend, for snubbing him by failing to light his cigarette. At least two bars revoked his drinking privileges for a time. He continued to play pool and shuffleboard for money, generally losing. He offered to pay his debts with real estate parcels, but most of the men he played wanted quick cash. One night he attempted to pull into a parking space in front of the Frontier Café. He misjudged his speed, the distance, and the road conditions, and plowed into the rear end of a parked car. The reaction of the people, even the tavern owners, was not expressed in terms of anger toward Dr. Hume. They understood what he had done for them professionally, and what he had gone through personally. But when he got that inebriated, he was a liability few of them could withstand.

His behavior even had an impact on his close friendship with Neal. Late one night, the doctor knocked on the front door of the Wright home. It was too late to be taking visitors, and Neal did not answer the knock. Dr. Hume knocked harder and began yelling too, but still Neal did not respond. Knowing Neal was inside, and not wanting to be ignored, the doctor picked up a nearby shovel and threw it through the door window. That was too much even for Neal to tolerate, and he became very upset, almost distraught. Dr. Hume knew he had stepped over the line with someone he needed very much. The next day a handyman replaced the broken window, and the doctor presented the Wrights with an expensive original Fred Machetanz oil painting as a peace offering. He had made a sincere effort to correct his wrongdoing, but Neal was getting ever more worried about his friend's erratic behavior.

Dr. Hume spent Christmas of 1968 with his family in Oregon, returning to Palmer shortly after the New Year. During his visit in Oregon, he didn't appear to be using any kind of prescription medication, but back in Palmer, he resumed his lifestyle of addiction.

A friend in Palmer was worried enough to telephone John Hume and inform him of his son's behavior and deep depression. The caller believed the doctor might be actively considering suicide. Not only was the caller a reliable source with genuine concern, but John Hume already had some personal knowledge of his son's emotional state. Eleven months earlier, when the elder Hume was in Alaska to attend Frank's funeral, he had taken a bottle of Percodan from him, which the doctor was considering using in a suicide attempt. So, John Hume called Myrt and told her of the latest crisis in Palmer. She was not altogether surprised, for she had sensed an emotional change in the doctor. He had written her letters that began just fine, but trailed off into nonsense. She imagined that whatever drug he was consuming overtook him by mid-letter, reducing his thoughts to gibberish. Worried about her husband, Myrt, along with their youngest child John, journeyed back to Palmer to assess the situation. She found that her father-in-law had been correctly informed. But her attempts to help her husband were thwarted by his absence; of the seven days she and John were in Palmer, the doctor was present to have dinner with them just once.

The only bright spot for Dr. Hume in the opening months of 1969 was that a new doctor was on his way to Palmer. The new physician arranged to lease the Hume office, freeing Dr. Hume to join his family in Oregon. Upon learning of his planned departure, community members planned a proper sendoff. As Dr. Hume packed for the move, he stopped long enough to thank his employees for their faithful service and present them with generous gifts. He also took time to treat the injured hand of a construction worker who happened by in the midst of the packing. His eleven years in Palmer, the longest he had ever lived in one place, were drawing to a close. A farewell dinner was held at the Elk's Lodge on February 21st. Shortly thereafter, on what must have been a late night of soul-searching, he called the hospital while completely sober and asked to speak to nurse Eleanor Brooks. She had long ago earned his respect. She was surprised to hear from him, and even more surprised when he asked for her opinion regarding his professional abilities. She told him the truth. She said he was a wonderful doctor and he had the respect of everyone in the healthcare profession when he was sober, but no one appreciated his drinking and it was unacceptable. He listened to her in silence, never interrupting to counter her or in any way defend himself. When she had finished speaking, he told her he appreciated her honesty, and then he said goodbye.

Oregon

Dr. Hume's arrival in Corvallis was met with well-warranted trepidation by his family. In short order they found he was still surrounded by chaos, and they feared that about him. His tone was still harsh, his tongue still a stinger. He confounded and confused them. Still, despite it all, they continued to love him. They held out hope that in the solace of his profession, he could break free of that which haunted him.

He tried to regain his footing in the medical community by applying to practice at Albany General Hospital, just north of Corvallis. When personnel from Albany General contacted the hospital in Palmer to reference his work record, they were told of the suspension. The Palmer hospital would not recommend his services. Taking heed, Albany General Hospital declined Dr. Hume's application for practice. There really wasn't much for him to do after that.

He was consuming an array of pills. Unable to procure them in the quantity he needed in Oregon, he had them shipped down in bulk from Palmer. He took Thorazine, often used in the treatment of schizophrenia, which as a side effect caused him involuntary spasms or twitches in his face. He took Dilaudid, a narcotic pain reliever that was highly addictive. And he took Seconal, another highly addictive drug used to relieve insomnia. Seconal was prescribed with caution for those suffering from severe depression and for those with a history of alcohol or drug abuse. Used in concert, these drugs caused Dr. Hume to ease into somewhat of a vegetative state. Often he didn't bother to get dressed, opting instead to lie around the house in a blue terrycloth robe.

On occasion he found the energy to get dressed for the day and go out for a round of golf. Sometimes he talked about reviving his career; perhaps they would buy that small rundown rest home near Sweethome. Once, he even talked himself into returning to Alaska to reclaim the place of his past glories. He set forth driving northward, but before he had traveled far, he got into a car accident and was forced to return to Corvallis.

Most of the time he mourned. He mourned the loss of his son. He mourned that he had not been a better father. He mourned that he had run out of options in the medical profession. In his more lucid moments, he was aware of his relentless cycle of despair and once even summoned the courage to confront it. He saw a medical doctor and confessed his emotional state. He asked the doctor's advice in seeking help from the psychiatric profession. For Dr. Hume to seek advice and to admit his weaknesses was a major step. On the question of help from the psychiatric profession, his colleague said, "Ah, Vince, those guys never helped anybody." And that was the end of that.

Brave faces all around. Dr. Hume, John, Starr, and Myrt. Back row: April, Dawn, and Cindy. (*Hume family collection*)

His family was completely unnerved by it all. Myrt prayed, and tried to hold it together. The girls weathered the storm as best they could, but they were under tremendous pressure, and cracks in the façade began to appear. Even when their father attempted to integrate himself into a normal family routine such as picking them up after school, he was generally so impaired that he frightened them on the way back to the farm. His father John was monitoring the situation through communications with Myrt. John strongly urged her to have the doctor committed, against his will, to a mental facility. That was easier said than done. Myrt knew if she had him committed, he would never forgive her for it. She even suspected that her safety might be in jeopardy if she did. But the situation was steadily worsening, and she made the decision. After the holidays, she would have her husband committed.

Christmas 1969

On Christmas day, Dr. Hume sat down to dinner in his robe, and ate like an animal. It was an embarrassing display. In front of the assembled guests and family, he shoveled down the food, seemingly oblivious to his surroundings. As Myrt passed by him, he stood and gave her a big hug and told her, "Things will be different after Christmas." He repeated it several times, "Things will be different after Christmas." That night, after he had gone to bed, Myrt went to check on him. She took the burning cigarette from his hand. He felt cold and didn't seem to be breathing. She got his stethoscope from his bag and listened for a heartbeat. Hearing none, she knew her husband was dead.

The Facts of the Matter

News of his death landed Dr. Hume on the front page of *The Frontiersman* one last time. The causes of death were erroneously reported as heart attack and pneumonia.

Services were conducted in Corvallis at the Mayflower Chapel, with the Reverend Joseph Jacobberger officiating. He was cremated and his ashes were later interred next to his son Frank in Palmer, Alaska.

As with much of his life, Dr. Hume remained a mystery in death. Did he die from an accidental overdose, or did he take his own life? The official cause of death was listed as barbiturate intoxication/suicide. Suicide would seem likely given the fact that he suffered from depression, suffered from addiction, and could be accurately described as a thoroughly defeated man. But he left no note, and therefore no one can ever be absolutely certain of his last intentions.

This much was certain, he died on December 26, 1969. He was preceded in death by his brother Frank and his son Frank. He was survived by his wife Myrtle, daughters April, Dawn, Cindy, and Starr, and son John. He was also survived by his father, John Hume, and his mother Clara Bates, as well as his sister Doreen, and his step-father Grover Bates. He was a gifted physician. He was 48 years old.

15

Aftermath

Searching For Answers

In the wake of human tragedy, victims and onlookers inevitably ask why. In the case of Dr. Hume, the question is encumbered by so many complex issues that formulating a single illuminating answer is difficult.

It is possible that medicine was a poor choice of professions for Dr. Hume, although the very thought would have been heresy to those he healed. He had difficulties maintaining the professional distance required in a doctor/patient relationship. No doubt he realized he couldn't cure everyone, but pain and suffering in others played upon his sensitive nature and produced in him an enormous sadness. The younger the patient, the more intense was his emotional reaction. Even when he was successful beyond all expectations, he felt himself lacking. In his greatest triumphs, he believed he should have done more. All of this left him emotionally bankrupt. Few other professions would have had such an effect.

Narcissistic traits may have motivated his entry into the medical field, traits developed from inconsistent acceptance from his parents and fear of abandonment. Becoming a physician provided him a seemingly endless supply of recognition, adoration, and status. But his drinking, and the disruption it caused, seemed to lessen and even undo some of his past achievements. The supply of recognition, adoration, and status was finally exhausted and replaced with pity. To a narcissist, the loss of reflected self-image is the ultimate failure.

The majority of the second half of the doctor's life was adversely impacted by his use of alcohol. By all accounts, even as late as his senior year at Baylor, he was considered only a light social drinker. It was during his stint in the Army Medical Corps that he began to overuse alcohol. How his consumption got beyond his control relatively quickly is uncertain. Perhaps the answer lies partly in heredity. His father John had problems with alcohol, but was able to overcome them. Gracie rarely drank, but she was known to overindulge when she did, which might be why she and Grover did not keep alcohol in their home. Whatever the reason, Dr. Hume was an alcoholic, and this addiction led to still others.

His motor vehicle accident on the Alaska Highway in December of 1965 began a significant downturn in his life. The nature of his injuries and the chronic pain that followed, prompted his use, then overuse, of prescription medicines. Already an addictive personality suffering from the compulsion to overwork, he was heavily dependent on alcohol, the universal gateway drug, so the addition of another addictive drug was, at least in retrospect, predictable. From the painkillers to the morphine to finally the barbiturates, the drugs that ultimately ended his life, all can be linked to that 1965 auto accident.

From Dr. Hume's earliest memories, it must have seemed to him that no one in authority conducted personal or professional business on the level. They didn't seem to suffer lasting repercussions for their transgressions, either. His father John married his mother, then abandoned her with three small children. His mother took up with and married a traveling salesman in Grover Bates. Gracie and Grover traveled far and wide, while the doctor and his siblings were foisted off in boarding schools, strangers' homes, and orphanages. The children's names were changed. The doctor's early years were rootless and lacking in stability. He attended seven schools in twelve years. While his parents pursued their own happiness, the children had no lasting friendships and no sense of belonging. Then, after Grover's arrest, the doctor found out what the authority figures in his life had *really* been up to—con games and eluding the law. He learned that rules didn't necessarily apply to everyone, maybe not to anyone.

His entry into the military as an officer, and especially as a physician, placed him outside the normal rigid code of discipline. He was granted wide personal latitude. Sometimes he must have felt untouchable. When he left the military, he journeyed to the Alaska frontier, the hinterlands of professional advancement. But one man's exile is another man's liberation. He ended up in Palmer, where people minded their own business and tended to look the other way. A place where one city councilman held elected office after serving time in a Federal penitentiary for embezzlement from a Palmer bank. If that wasn't unabashed flaunting of authority, what was? Dr. Hume had found a place to put down roots, a place to call home with few restrictions on personal or professional behavior. But Palmer started to grow up, and times changed. Dr. Hume's bad behaviors, which progressed with his disease, were no longer condoned. The position which once allowed him to do as he pleased now called for behavior above reproach. He found himself being judged by those generally beneath him in social status; they were acting as his authority figures. And, based on Dr. Hume's past experiences, authority figures were not worthy of much respect, and in no case were they to be taken seriously.

Having been a big fish in a little pond for so long, he must have thought he was impervious to any lasting personnel action. He had been able to work his first hospital suspension into a seamless vacation, and few were the wiser. Information on that event, like so many other escapades, had been handled on a need-to-know basis. His attitude made him blatantly defiant and allowed him to overplay his hand. That attitude played a significant role in his final suspension. Then, after he had moved to Oregon and applied for hospital privileges there, a call to Palmer for a recommendation sank his chances for good. That was a jolt of reality. The unwritten rules of the profession stated that such matters weren't supposed to follow you around.

Then came the pain no parent can ever totally conquer. He lost a son. Though most parents are somehow able to find the courage to carry on, Dr. Hume, already in a weak condition from fighting addiction and diminished by his professional humiliation, could not see past his pain.

And so, a single life-altering event does not exist. Instead, the totality of Dr. Hume's life holds the best answer as to why. His was a lifetime of incremental extremes, devoid of balance.

Changing Times

Not so long ago, almost any mother and father would have been overjoyed if one of their children had entered the medical profession. Not so much anymore. The national attitude has changed in its view of healthcare workers. Nurses have largely held their ground in public opinion, while hospital administrators, insurance companies, and doctors have seen a steady decline in approval numbers. Some of that decline may result from high-profile malpractice suits and negative portrayal of doctors in movies and television, but the public's displeasure also comes from firsthand experience. Doctors are said to be in too much of a hurry and that they don't listen. Both complaints contribute to a growing sense that doctors don't care anymore.

Doctors have been distracted by a growing number of governmental and institutional rules and regulations. They are further burdened by a litigious society that increases their insurance costs and drives some of their colleagues out of practice altogether. And it is probably true that doctors don't listen as well as they used to, relying instead on a bevy of high-tech equipment to assist them with diagnoses. That doesn't mean doctors don't care, it's just getting harder to tell that they do.

In the last forty years, the public's view of doctors has seen polar extremes. Where once they were considered to be warm fatherly figures, directly imbued with healing gifts from God, now they are often tagged as cold, uncaring, and unfeeling clinicians. The pendulum didn't even slow near the center, at humanity. Doctors are surprisingly human. From the mysticism that used to surround their profession, to the gee-whiz wonders of modern technology, they were never more or less than that.

More Changes

The profession has changed in other ways too. Medical students' interests have shifted from general practice to specialization. Specialization offers regular working hours and at least a chance of a normal life outside the profession. Who can blame them?

The medical profession has increased its efforts in policing its own. This remains a conflicted and difficult task, the results of which are hard to measure and impossible to report.

Occupational stress is addressed in medical school now, too.

Feelings and grief are open subjects. People aren't expected to "buck up" liked they used to.

Palmer

For the largest segment of the population of the Matanuska Valley, what was once the road to Palmer is now the road to Wasilla. Few would have predicted in Dr. Hume's time that Wasilla would surpass Palmer in population, but it did, and the current numbers aren't even close. For awhile, Palmer folks were somewhat bitter about that. After all the struggles the residents of Palmer endured, Wasilla ballooned with people, businesses, and skyrocketing property values. But most of the resentment has subsided. Part of growing up is acceptance and appreciation; in that way Palmer has achieved what few communities do—a measure of peace and contentment.

After Dr. Hume left Palmer, the severe shortage of doctors remained, and unprecedented efforts were undertaken to lure and keep doctors in the area. Now, scores of doctors serve the valley, but with the drastic increase in population, residents still grumble about the availability of open appointments.

The hospital where Dr. Hume worked in Palmer is no more. Mat-Su Regional Medical Center, a brand new thoroughly-modern facility near the Glenn and Parks Highway interchange, took its place in 2006.

The People

Neal Wright passed away in the early spring of 1989. His ashes were spread by plane over his drugstore and home in downtown Palmer.

The Mason LaZelle Memorial Award was established and is the highest honor bestowed by the Alaska Rural Electric Cooperative Association.

No lawsuits were filed by surviving family members of the 1968 MEA plane crash.

The nurses who served at the hospital with Dr. Hume still maintain their camaraderie. Each summer they convene for lunch to update one another on the latest events of their lives and share recollections from the past.

The hospital board members who held office during Dr. Hume's suspension remain mixed in their emotions of that time.

Some wish to keep the matter in the distant past and decline to discuss it. Others are more philosophical, reasoning it is all a matter of history now, and are willing to discuss their past service openly. Feelings in both camps are understandable.

Of all participants in the Hume story, perhaps the individual carrying the greatest burden has been Raymond Fuller. No one finds this more lamentable than Myrt and her daughters. The Hume women have expressed sincere caring for Raymond, their speech often choked with emotion when voicing concern for his well-being. Perhaps the depth of those feelings will someday bring comfort to Raymond.

It's a Wonderful Life

A number of parallels can be seen between the Frank Capra movie and Dr. Hume's life. Mary Beth Bouwens, so badly injured in a farm accident, is a married mother of three and a grandmother.

Eric Hollembaek lives near Delta Junction and is a well-thought-of man who, despite the distance, maintains friendships in Palmer. Scott Hollembaek, who pulled Eric from the dog lot so many years ago, sees Eric often and remains thankful to Dr. Hume for keeping his baby brother alive.

Bobby Blunt, the eleven-year-old boy Vinnie pulled from the Brackenridge Park pool in San Antonio, later saved another boy from drowning in the same pool. Bobby is the proud patriarch of a family that includes eight children, six grandchildren, and one great grandchild.

For Jimmy Smith, the Vinnie's high school chum and college roommate, hearing news of his old friend's medical achievements was heartening. Jimmy, who holds the principal values of hard work and the fruits of that labor dear, expressed pleasure that Vinnie had done good and important work.

The Humes

Clara "Gracie" Bates died in July of 1978. She and Grover had been married for forty-three years. Grover, who had been unquestionably devoted to her, was heartbroken; he died in November of the same year.

Dr. Hume's father, John, lived to the age of 91, passing away in June, 1990.

Doreen was angry at her brother for nearly a decade after his passing—resentful that he had either by his own hand or through carelessness, allowed himself to die. As she lay dying in 2002, she said she saw him again.

For her remaining years in high school, the girl who received her first kiss from Frank Hume made a pilgrimage to his gravesite every year at Easter. In his memory, Frank's classmates purchased a stone lithograph of artist Fred Machetanz's *Moose Tracks*, which fittingly depicts a lone hunter following animal tracks across a wintry landscape. The lithograph, with accompanying dedication, is on display at Palmer High School.

Two years after the doctor died, Myrt remarried. She was widowed for the second time in 1994. She now resides in New Iberia, Louisiana, which puts her in proximity to her daughter Dawn, and nearer to family members in Texas. Myrt remains a staunch champion for her children. She still speaks her mind. She has no illusions about her marriage to Dr. Hume, and her recollections of their years together are related with unblinking and uncompromising honesty. Surprisingly, she harbors little bitterness. She believes she has had a wonderful life.

Myrt's offspring recognize their mother's role as the anchor of the family. They know she took the brunt of the daily dose of chaos. She could have traveled the path of least resistance and taken up drinking with her husband, a move that might have afforded her some marital harmony. The kids know their lives would have been immeasurably different had that occurred, and they appreciate their mother's steadfastness.

The girls' recollections of life with their father are as complicated as the man himself. They can recall the power of his personality and his great intellect. They can also recall the searing pain his words inflicted, a pain that is real and with them even today. Despite the chaos and tears, the girls grew into strong, though sometimes fragile, intelligent women. It is regrettable that his daughters and youngest son didn't have more time with their father, just as it is unfortunate he didn't live to see to them reach adulthood with families of their own. As any father knows, his was the greater loss.

The Log House
The Hume's home in Palmer, which also served as the doc-

tor's office, has gone through a number of owners since the family left Palmer. Invariably, each summer as the present occupants are engaged in some outdoor chore, they notice cars driving by the house a little more slowly than necessary. On occasion, drivers will stop and come over—a little sheepishly at first—and launch into a story about this family, the Humes, that used to live there. About how smart and beautiful the girls were, and how the oldest boy was about the nicest kid around. They relate how the lady of the house, Mrs. Hume, was a tall, beautiful woman. She had a bit of an accent, and she looked so elegant driving around in that Caddy. They talk about the doctor, Doc Hume they call him, and about their memories of the downstairs office with that sailfish on the wall. Not wanting to sound too gushing, they say that the doctor had "a bit of a drinking problem," but they don't want to sound disrespectful either, so they add that a lot of people walking around Palmer today wouldn't be here if it weren't for Doc Hume. Then, realizing that perhaps they have rattled on a bit, they begin to retreat back to their car. As they walk away, they almost always look back and explain why they stopped in the first place. They explain that because the Humes were so important to Palmer, maybe those living in the Hume home would want to know.

Selected Bibliography

The following is a sampling of the works and sources consulted in the research for this book.

Alaska Medicine 1 (March 1959): 1 – 40.

Alaska State Trooper Report No. A-47458 and No. A-30966.

American & Canada Census Records 1890 – 1930.

Attorney General of British Columbia Case File Nos. C-95-4, C-95-4-38, and C-280-1/37.

Beare, Virginia, *Looking Back at the Old Hot Wells School*, Southside Reporter (San Antonio) 19 September 1996, Page 6.

City of Vancouver, British Columbia Police Court Calendar Entry No. 14838 and Court Documents.

Clark, S.J. Duncan et al.: *History's Greatest War*. E.T. Townsend: 1919.

Coombs, Robert Holman: *Drug – Impaired Professionals*. Cambridge, Massachusetts: Harvard University Press; 1997.

Fox, James H.: *The First Summer*. Palmer, Alaska: The Alaska Rural Rehabilitation Corporation; 1980.

Frances M.D., Allen et al.: *Diagnostic and Statistical Manual of Mental Disorders*. Washington, D.C.: American Psychiatric Association; 1999.

Frances Schupp vs Vincent Hume, Court File No. 62-77, 1962, State of Alaska, Third Judicial District (Palmer, Alaska).

Frontiersman (Alaska), The: 28 February 1952 - 11 October 1973.

Harvest of Memories, prod. by Sundance Productions, Maski-Pitoon

Historical Society and dir. Chad Anderson, 58 min., Sundance Productions, 2000, videocassette.

Huff, Barbara B. et al.: *Physicians' Desk Reference*. New Jersey: Litton Publications; 1970.

Hume family private papers. Canada and United States.

Johnson, Hugh A. and Keith L. Stanton: *Matanuska Valley Memoir: The Story of How One Alaskan Community Developed*. Alaska: University of Alaska; 1955.

Jordan, Nancy: *Frontier Physician: The Life and Legacy of Dr. C. Earl Albrecht*. Fairbanks, Alaska: Epicenter Press; 1996.

Los Angeles Times: 24 October 1938.

Moursund M.D., Walter H.: *A History of Baylor University College of Medicine 1900 – 1953*. Houston, Texas: Gulf Printing Company; 1956.

National Transportation Safety Board. NTSB Identification: AN-C68A0040. 14 CFR Part 91 General Aviation. Aircraft accident report for event of February 27, 1968.

Nolen M.D., William A.: *The Making of a Surgeon*. New York, New York: Random House; 1970.

San Antonio Express: 23 October 1938 – 22 August 1939.

San Antonio Light: 23 – 27 October 1938.

United States Army Records Center, St. Louis, Missouri, Military Records of Vincent Hume.

United States Case File No. Le 211.42 Bates, Grover J. /5 and /1.

Vancouver Daily Province: 1935 – 1939.

Vancouver Sun: 1935 – 1939.

Acknowledgments

I initially contacted the Hume family to request permission and cooperation in telling Dr. Hume's story. I received a lot more than that. Myrt and the girls spoke with unflinching openness about the triumphs, trials, and tragedies of their family. They never lost patience with my incessant questioning, and even offered encouragement along the way. What did they want in return? In the beginning, Myrt asked that I tell the truth about her husband. That was all she ever asked, and she only asked once. The trust the Hume family placed in me, with no prior knowledge of my ethics or character, is beyond my comprehension. They will be with me always.

From my first interviews, it was obvious that nearly forty years after his passing, Dr. Hume's name continued to provoke strong recollections and passionate opinions from his contemporaries. There were few fence-sitters on the subject of Dr. Hume. Of the more than 150 people who were asked for interviews, only three declined. Most who did contribute asked not to be quoted or even acknowledged for their contributions. In honoring this request, no individual citations have been made. All of the contributions were important. The memories and insights provided by Dr. Hume's high school, college, and medical school classmates were substantial, and I am grateful for their help. I'm also grateful to the people of Palmer, past community leaders, those associated with the hospital, the Hume's friends and neighbors, and the classmates of the Hume children. To their credit, they all requested the story be told with care and sensitivity.

The Frontiersman allowed me great access to their newspaper archives, indispensable in the research of this book. Newspaper research of another kind was conducted by my brother, Jordon Weekes, in Austin, Texas. Armed with almost no date information to narrow his search, he scanned 1930s San Antonio newspapers and located a small news item concerning Dr. Hume's step-father. It was a find that led to the uncovering of still more and tremendously important information concerning the doctor's early life.

In addition to those who contributed their recollections and insights into the life and times of Dr. Hume were those who aided me through their support and encouragement. Thank you.

Thanks also to Lorie Kirker, Lynette Lehn, Ingrid Youngs, Rory Redick, Sherri Spangler, Mike Stewart, Darleen Stoepler, Sheila Homme, and Ed Homme, who braved reading the early draft of the story and for offering such constructive comments.

A special thank you to Dave Filucci, Jim Fox, and the always-faithful Carol Seidlitz, who went above and beyond the call of friendship and offered great assistance in shaping and editing the text.

Finally, my family is deserving of thanks for enduring yet another project in good humor. In particular my wife, Cheryl, who is the hardest working person I have ever known, provided her usual steadfast help and support in the realization of my ambitions.

About the Author

Joe Homme was born in Palmer, Alaska in April of 1959 and was delivered by Dr. Vincent Hume, the subject of this book. Joe grew up in Palmer and currently resides there with his wife Cheryl and son James.

Also by Joseph Homme

Storybook Culture: The Art of Popular Children's Books

Retro Romance: Classic Tips for Today's Couple

Additional copies of *Cures and Chaos,* and thousands
of other Alaska titles, may be purchased from:

Alaskana Books
564 S. Denali St.
Palmer, AK 99645
Toll free phone: 1-888-354-9483
e-mail: alaskanabooks@alaska.com